LIFE ADVICE FOR TEENS

Important Stuff Every Teenager
Should Know in Life!

Susan Burke

ISBN: 978-1-962496-07-0

For questions, please reach out to Support@OakHarborPress.com

Please consider leaving a review!

Just visit: OakHarborPress.com/Reviews

FREE BONUS

SCAN ME!

GET OUR NEXT BOOK FOR FREE!

Scan or go to:

OakHarborPress.com/Free

TABLE OF CONTENTS

INTRODUCTION

Life can be challenging, especially during your teenage years when much seems uncertain and overwhelming. Your teens are a time of self-discovery, development, and change, but they can also be a time of anxiety and confusion. You may be perplexed by matters like your relationships with peers, your personality, and the future. As a result, you can be tempted to make hasty decisions with long-term consequences. *Life Advice for Teens* is specially written for you to help you navigate this critical stage of your life.

This book is a comprehensive manual that provides you with practical counsel, helpful hints, and insightful guidelines to help you through life's ups and downs. You may suffer from low self-esteem and be worried about your body, how you look, family issues, relationship issues, academic performance, and peer pressure, or you may simply be trying to find your place in life.

Life Advice for Teens provides you with the tools you need to succeed and thrive, from developing healthy habits and setting goals to coping with stress and building meaningful relationships. This book also touches on principles and etiquette to help you to develop a strong moral compass. In addition, it teaches you how to cultivate and show gratitude, prioritize your health, and practice self-care in order to lead a more fulfilling and productive life.

This book is intended to be engaging and accessible to readers of all backgrounds and experiences, with clear and concise language, relatable examples, and practical activities at the end of each chapter. It's a book that you can return to again and again as you navigate life's challenges during these formative years. *Life Advice for Teens* is the book for you, whether you're seeking advice, inspiration, or just a friendly voice to support you along the road.

CHAPTER ONE: SETTING GOALS

If you feel like you're just going through the motions of everyday life or you're struggling with a sense of direction, it will benefit you to make a plan of action. Maybe you have big dreams and aspirations, but you're unsure how to make them happen. This chapter will guide you through how to set goals and design your life with intention.

Setting goals isn't just about being productive; it's about having a positive mindset and working toward something you really want. When you have a goal in mind, you're more likely to take actions that will help you achieve it. Accomplishing goals grants a sense of purpose and control over your life. It can help build self-efficacy, which is your confidence in your ability to achieve whatever you put your mind to.

MAINTAINING A POSITIVE MINDSET

A positive mindset will help you keep focused and on track as you work on achieving your goals. No matter how good you are at something, challenges will eventually arise that will test your commitment. Recognizing that every failure is a lesson, not a reflection of your worth, is important to maintaining a positive outlook even when things aren't going as planned.

The Importance of Keeping a Positive Mindset

How you speak to yourself internally will affect how you see problems and obstacles when they arise. Speaking to yourself in an uplifting and encouraging manner will prevent you from getting discouraged. Instead of saying things like, "I can't do this," or "I'm not good enough," try saying, "I can do this if I give it my all," or "I have what it takes to achieve great things." It may feel silly at first, but positive self-talk can help you develop a more confident and optimistic attitude over time.

Cultivating a positive mindset takes practice. For many people, it doesn't come naturally. It requires intentionally choosing your thoughts and re-training old thought patterns. A couple ways to do this include:

Focusing on your strengths. Whenever you catch yourself fretting about your weaknesses or perceived failures, try to repeat three things you're good at to help counteract it. This can feel awkward at first, but eventually it will become a habit.

Practice gratitude. Gratitude focuses your thoughts on neutral things outside of yourself. Instead of focusing on good and bad perceptions, it allows you to concentrate on real, tangible things. Even listing mundane or silly aspects of your life is helpful. For example, if you have a bad day, you might write a list with the following thoughts: *I am grateful for my pets. I am grateful I have food* *to eat. I am grateful for this class.* Some days, you'll have deeper thoughts than others, but the important part is to practice. Keeping a journal and writing out these lists daily will help you develop a good habit.

It's important to remember that having a positive mindset doesn't guarantee you won't face challenges or setbacks. Everyone experiences failures and obstacles at some point, but it's how you respond to them that matters; instead of giving up or getting discouraged, make an effort to focus on the lessons learned from the experience.

IMPORTANCE OF SETTING GOALS

Learning how to set realistic goals takes practice. When done right, you'll be able to focus your energy and effectively prioritize tasks to achieve a specific outcome. Aside from producing results, learning to achieve goals will help you follow through with tasks despite setbacks or a loss of motivation. Goals are important for accomplishing anything, whether it's something personal, educational, or even work related. Every time you accomplish a small step toward a bigger vision, you work on building confidence in your abilities. When you create effective goals, you'll have big dreams and then smaller tasks to help you get there. In this chapter, we'll cover how to create a plan for success and track your progress for best results.

DIFFERENT TYPES OF GOALS

As a teen, you have your whole life ahead of you, and setting goals is one of the best ways to create a life you love. You might be at a loss about what goals you should set, but that's okay! Here are some ideas to get you started:

Academic goals: Setting academic goals might start with a grand vision such as earning a 4.0 GPA or receiving a full-ride scholarship to a good university. Smaller tasks to meet this goal could include things like finishing all your homework on time and getting to every class early.

Personal development goals: These goals can be anything, really. Whether it's starting a new exercise program or keeping a gratitude journal, these goals are meant to help you build a happy, fulfilling life. It's not a good idea to start too many of these at once since that can become overwhelming! Focus on building one new habit at a time, and when it's routine and easy to maintain, set another goal.

Career goals: Setting goals based on the career you want is important for success in the future. This stage of life is the perfect time to think about what brings you true joy in the world. You have plenty of time to be more realistic or analytical about your career choices, but for now, set your vision on your dream job! A big goal might include becoming a famous artist, while a small goal could be drawing one small picture every day.

Financial goals: Financial goals are crucial for stability, security, and peace of mind. If you want to save up for a car, setting a budget allows you to make progress toward that larger goal over time.

Social goals: Social goals are essential for building a solid support network and deepening your connections with others. These goals can include making new friends, working to improve your communication skills, or becoming more involved in your community.

Whether you're dreaming big or just trying to get through the day, setting goals will help you achieve your dreams and become the best version of yourself. You can create a fulfilling, meaningful, and unique life by setting different goals and working towards them consistently.

STRATEGIES FOR ACHIEVING GOALS

There are a lot of resources out there to help you develop and accomplish goals. Online videos, teachers, and books are all great places to start learning more. Below, we've created simplified guidelines for achieving your dreams.

Create a vision. Start with a daydream. Imagine the life you want 1 year and 10 years from now. Dream big; don't set any limits for yourself right now. Maybe you have a specific vision for how you want to look, what kind of friendships you'd like, where you want to go to school, or the kind of lifestyle you'd like to live. At this stage, you don't need to be realistic; you just need to know what you want.

Think about your habits. Once you have a better idea of who you want to be and what kind of life you want to live, consider what daily habits will help you create this vision. This might require research. For example, if you want to become a millionaire, you should spend some time researching the habits millionaires practice daily. This may seem like an unrealistic goal, but working to build these habits early on will bring you closer to achieving that goal than just hoping it'll happen someday. If you want to earn a scholarship, you have to build good study habits. If you want to run a marathon, you'll need to make a habit of running and strength training. Habits take time to cultivate, but fully integrating them into your routine is the best way to progress toward big dreams with minimal effort. The hardest part of this step is identifying which habits you want to cultivate and then starting them.

Break down goals into smaller tasks. While a vision can be a broad—and oftentimes vague—concept, your goals should be concrete steps. For example, if you dream of backpacking in a foreign country after high school, start by figuring out how much it costs, what paperwork you'll need, and the specific places you want to go. Once you identify these things, you can break down each of these into smaller tasks and habits. A habit might include keeping a budget or showing up five minutes early to every scheduled shift at a part-time job. A task might include saving a specific amount of money by next year or applying for your passport. Breaking your goals down into smaller tasks will make each goal less overwhelming.

Set completion dates for your goals. It's easier to stay on track if you set a schedule for when you want to achieve each goal or task. If you want to run a marathon, you could look up the dates for marathons hosted nearby and use them to create a schedule. It's okay if you don't make it by your original deadline. You can use that point to reassess your process by returning to these steps and making adjustments.

Record your progress. One of the most important things about setting and achieving goals is learning what works for you—and what doesn't. While your friend might study really well in the morning, you might not be a morning person and discover you work best after dinner. By recording your progress, you'll be able to identify where you need to modify your process. If you set a financial goal and don't make it, having a record of your spending will allow you to set a more realistic goal. Maybe you underestimated how much gas you actually use or overestimated how much money you earn. Identifying where to make changes is an important part of the process.

Stay motivated. It's really easy to lose motivation over time. Usually, people will feel highly motivated during the early stages of pursuing a dream, then once they hit an obstacle or a plateau in their process, their motivation wavers. This is perfectly normal! One of the ways to stay focused on the bigger picture is by recalling your original vision whenever you start to feel like giving up. Another technique is to surround yourself with media (e.g., posters, videos, etc.) that inspires you to achieve your goal. You can also enlist the help of friends, family, mentors, or online communities with the same goals. The more you surround yourself with things and people that inspire you, the easier it is to stay motivated when things get tough.

Be consistent. Consistency is key to achieving your goals. Sometimes, you will fall out of practice with a habit or a goal, and that's okay. However, it's important to start again as soon as you recognize that you're off track. For example, if you set exercise goals and then get sick and have to stop for two weeks, this might temporarily throw you off track. Life happens! Once you start feeling better, though, pick up where you left off and keep going.

Celebrate your successes. Setting rewards for milestones is important. It can also be helpful to pick rewards that align with your goals. If you finish all your homework successfully for two weeks, rewarding yourself by skipping a study session isn't helpful. Instead, pick something that adds to your life without undermining your success. Some good things might include spending extra time on self-care, scheduling an outing with some friends, or throwing a small celebration with family.

Setting and achieving goals is a lifelong practice. The more you learn through trial and error, the stronger your belief in yourself will be. Eventually, it will be easier to see large tasks through. Remember that there's no one-size-fits-all method to achieve a goal or dream; it requires learning about yourself and what works for you.

ACTIVITY: CREATING A VISION BOARD

Creating a vision board is a great way to identify your big dreams and keep you motivated on your journey.

Gather your materials. You'll need a poster board or canvas, magazines, scissors, glue, and any other art supplies you want to use, such as markers or stickers. You can also do this on your phone or by putting pictures on your bedroom wall (with permission from your guardian).

Set your intention. What are your long- and short-term goals?

Collect images and words. Flip through magazines and cut out images and words that resonate with your intentions and goals.

Arrange your images. Start arranging your images on your poster board or canvas. You can organize them by theme or just arrange them in a visually appealing way.

Glue everything down. Once you're happy with the layout of your images, glue everything down. If you're decorating your bedroom with inspiring images, you can use tape or tacks depending on what your guardian allows.

Display your vision board. Hang the finished product somewhere you'll see it every day, such as in your bedroom or at your desk. Look at your vision board daily and visualize your intentions and goals coming true. Focusing on the happy feelings this daydream creates for you makes you more likely to take steps toward achieving it.

CHAPTER TWO: MANAGING TIME EFFECTIVELY

Everyone struggles to find balance between all their responsibilities and aspirations at some point or another. Learning healthy time-management skills is another important part of creating a happy life. It takes practice, though, to figure out what works best for you; keep in mind that your process might change periodically throughout your life.

Time management is all about organizing and planning how you spend your time on various activities. It may seem daunting at first, but once you learn how to manage your time effectively, you'll be more productive with less stress. When you don't plan your schedule out, it's easy to miss deadlines or become overwhelmed by what's on your plate.

THE IMPORTANCE OF TIME MANAGEMENT

Creating a schedule to manage your time might seem rigid or restrictive, but it actually creates more freedom for you to do the things you love most. It can also decrease anxiety. If you know when you're going to handle your responsibilities, you'll be able to relax the rest of the time. Here are some other benefits to building healthy time management skills:

Increased productivity: By creating a plan for when you'll accomplish your goals, you're more likely to follow through without excessive stress. If you don't know when you'll complete a task, you could end up worrying about it when you're having fun or rushing to complete it at the last minute.

Improved quality of work: By giving yourself enough time to complete tasks, you can produce higher-quality work that meets or exceeds expectations. Effective time management also allows you to review your work and make any necessary revisions.

More personal time: Proper time management allows you to pursue your hobbies, spend time with your loved ones, or just relax. This can help you achieve a better work-life balance and improve your overall happiness.

More opportunities: When you manage your time well, you can easily take on new projects or activities without feeling overwhelmed or stressed. This can help you grow and develop new skills or plan fun events with your favorite people.

Better reputation: By consistently meeting deadlines and producing high-quality work, you can build a reputation for reliability and excellence among your friends and peers.

TECHNIQUES FOR TIME MANAGEMENT

There are many ways to achieve a healthy balance in your schedule. One piece of advice you will read repeatedly in this book is to use multiple resources while trying to figure out what works best for you. These can include family members, peers, teachers, or forms of media like online videos. Some tips for developing a good sense of balanced time management are below.

Time-Log Exercise

A time-log exercise involves keeping track of your activities throughout the day and categorizing them into different groups such as work, leisure, and personal care. By analyzing your time log, you can identify time-wasting activities, prioritize your tasks, and evaluate the effectiveness of your routines.

Start by recording all your activities throughout the day. It's essential to be honest and accurate while logging your activities as this will help you identify patterns and areas for improvement. It's also a good idea to time yourself performing these tasks. You might be surprised to find that doing the dishes takes much less time than you think it does. Meanwhile, scrolling on your phone could be taking up a huge chunk of your free time without you noticing. You can write these down in a journal or the notes app on your phone. Once you have a couple days of data, ask yourself these questions:

- *How much time do I spend on work?*

- *How much time do I spend on leisure?*

- *How much time do I spend on personal care?*

- *What are my most time-consuming activities?*

- *What are my biggest wastes of time?*

- *Do I spend enough time on important activities?*

By answering these questions, you can identify where you want to make improvements and how much time tasks actually take.

Prioritization

Prioritization is an essential component of effective time management. It involves determining which tasks or activities are most important to finish first. To prioritize tasks, create a to-do list. Identify which tasks happen every day (your habits), which tasks have a deadline, and which tasks are unimportant. It's a good idea to rank your obligations in time order. For example, you might have homework to complete for the next day. That's a high-priority task, and the faster you knock it out, the sooner you can relax. Catching up on a television show is probably an unimportant task (unless it's self-care or a show you truly love) because time-wasting activities often take away from the things you love the most. Some chores are important to complete but can wait for later. This category might include things like reorganizing your closet.

ELIMINATING TIME-WASTING HABITS

Identifying and eliminating time-wasting habits can help you make more room for what you truly desire for yourself. Every time you say *yes* to something, you're saying *no* to something else. If you decide to scroll on your phone, you might not have time to get your homework done and still hang out with your friends on the weekend. By the time you complete the exercises listed above, you should have a good idea of how you're wasting time. Although you don't need to get rid of every activity that doesn't add value to your life, it's a good idea to indulge in them in moderation.

Bundle your time. Mixing time-wasting activities with more productive tasks can be helpful at times. Putting a movie on while you clean your room can make the experience a little more enjoyable. You could also talk to your friend on the phone while you finish an easy task that you don't really have to think about (e.g., sweeping the floor).

Create a schedule. This is an essential step in effective time management. To create a schedule, identify your most critical tasks and commitments, such as work, school, or household duties. Block out time for these activities first, ensuring that you have enough time to complete them without feeling rushed or stressed. Keep in mind that self-care and leisure are just as important as finishing your chores or homework. It is also a good idea to create "buffer" time around tasks; allowing an extra 15 to 30 minutes for every task gives you a little wiggle room for life to happen. If you don't need the extra time to complete the task, you can use it for something you love at the end of the day.

Eliminate distractions. Identify time-wasting activities and temptations such as texting, online videos, social media, or spending too much time with friends. You can avoid getting distracted by planning ahead. For example, it might be a good idea to put your phone on silent and stick it in a drawer while studying.

Setting boundaries and communicating with others in a healthy way can be difficult, and it takes practice to find the right rhythm. Let your family and friends know when you've scheduled certain tasks. You can even consider making them a part of your planning.

By letting them know in advance how you intend to use your time, it's less likely that they'll interrupt you accidentally.

Track your progress. Keeping a record of how far you've come isn't just a good idea for goal setting. It can also help you keep an eye on time-management habits. If you cut too much fun out of your life in the name of productivity, you might start to feel burned out. By keeping a journal of how you feel and what's working, you can steadily create a balanced schedule that leaves you feeling accomplished and relaxed.

ACTIVITY: CREATING A SCHEDULE

After completing the exercises above, you'll be ready to create your first schedule. It's important to keep in mind that this is a work in progress. Your first plan might not work that well for you, and that's okay. Take it slow. Once you create your first schedule, give yourself an adjustment period while you record how you feel and make any other observations. Come back and tweak it until you've created something that really works for you.

Here are some things to consider:

- Are you a morning or night person?
- What times of day do you have the lowest energy?
- How would you like to spend your free time?
- What makes you the happiest?

- Which tasks are the hardest?

Create a time log based on this sample.

Note that this is just an example to guide you. You may wake up at 4 a.m. and have your breakfast at 10 a.m. Make sure to follow what works best for you.

6:00 a.m. — Waking up and getting ready for the day

7:00 a.m. — Breakfast

8:00 a.m. — School

3:00 p.m. — Homework/study time

4:30 p.m. — Exercise (30 minutes)

5:00 p.m. — Dinner

6:00 p.m. — Free time

9:00 p.m. — Bedtime

CHAPTER THREE:
BUILDING HEALTHY
HABITS

Research has shown that there are only so many decisions a person is capable of making each day. This is why it's easy to make good choices at the beginning of the day, but your motivation and discernment decline toward the end of the day. Building healthy habits into your routine helps eliminate some of these choices by making certain aspects of your day automatic. For example, if every day you wake up and immediately go to the bathroom to complete a hygiene routine, that habit can eventually occur on autopilot. This is why building good habits is so important.

Earlier, we briefly discussed how cultivating good habits can help you achieve your best life. This chapter takes a deeper dive into what that means and how you can build healthy habits into your daily routine.

THE BENEFITS OF HEALTHY HABITS

Healthy habits are whatever actions you consistently take to improve your life. They're usually small efforts ingrained into your routine. Just as there are good habits, there are also bad habits. A good habit might include brushing your teeth, completing a workout routine, or picking up your room. A bad habit could be opening your phone as soon as you wake up to check social media or waiting to do your homework until right before it's due. Listed below are some ways that developing healthy habits can change your life.

Improved physical health. One of the most significant benefits of healthy habits is improved physical health. Engaging in regular exercise, eating a nutritious diet, getting enough sleep, and practicing good hygiene will help keep your body running in tip-top shape.

Enhanced mental health. Healthy habits can also positively impact your mental health. The more helpful habits you add to your routine, the less you need to think about your day, which can decrease anxiety. There are other chain reactions as well. If you practice a good sleep routine, you'll feel better throughout the day. If you practice completing your homework as soon as it's assigned, you'll avoid a stressful rush to finish everything in time.

Improved productivity. When you care for your body and mind, you'll likely be more productive and focused in other areas of your life. Regular exercise and healthy eating can give you the energy and mental clarity to tackle your daily tasks more efficiently.

Increased self-esteem. When you feel physically and mentally well, you're more likely to have high self-esteem. You can boost your self-confidence and feel more comfortable in your own skin by engaging in healthy habits.

STRATEGIES FOR BUILDING HEALTHY HABITS

It's difficult to make or break habits once they're established. If you've identified areas where you want to improve, there are easy ways to make the process more manageable. Check out these tips for building healthy habits that will work for you:

Start small: Trying to introduce too many changes at once can be overwhelming and may make it challenging to stick to your new habits. Instead, start with one small change at a time. If you want to exercise more, start with 10 minutes a day and gradually work your way up. Focus on one habit at a time.

Make a plan: Decide when and where to engage in your new habit. Linking new habits to an already established one increases your chances of success. If you want to read more, you can link that habit to anytime you're waiting in line or stuck between classes. If you want to improve your hygiene routine, you can link it to your morning bathroom break.

Track your progress: Tracking progress is an important part of recognizing patterns. It can also increase your motivation since you can look back and see how much you've changed since starting your journey.

Find a support system: Having support from friends, family, or a mentor can make it easier to stick to your new habit. Joining a fitness class or finding a workout buddy, for example, can help keep you accountable.

Celebrate your successes: Rewarding yourself when you succeed, no matter how small the victory, can help you stay motivated and reinforce the positive changes you're making.

Practice self-compassion: It's essential to be kind to yourself and practice self-compassion when building healthy habits. If you slip up or miss a day, don't beat yourself up. Instead, recommit to your goal and keep trying.

Using these strategies, you can build healthy habits that will last a lifetime. Remember, creating healthy habits is a journey, not a destination! Be patient, persistent, and consistent; you'll be well on your way to a healthier and happier you.

IDENTIFYING UNHEALTHY HABITS

Unhealthy habits don't bring you closer toward your ideal vision for your life. Everyone has good and bad habits, but good habits are those that help you maintain a healthy lifestyle.

Identifying Unhealthy Habits

Be honest with yourself. Don't make excuses or minimize a bad habit's impact on your life. One way to identify a bad habit is by asking yourself if a habit helps you reach your goals or distracts you from them. While sleeping in one day won't negatively your goals, you can't ignore your homework because you'd rather take a nap every night after school.

Keep a journal. One effective way to identify unhealthy habits is to keep a journal. Write the habits you want to change and the situations that trigger them. For example, if you're going to stop snacking late at night, write down what triggers your desire to snack, such as being bored, stressed, sad, or tired.

Seek feedback. Ask your friends, family, or a trusted professional about your habits. They may be able to point out habits that you're unaware of. Sometimes, others see what you cannot see in yourself. Remember not to take these observations personally, though! Everyone has bad habits; it's not a reflection of your worth.

Eliminating Unhealthy Habits

Unhealthy habits can hurt your physical and mental health, making it harder to reach your goals. After you've identified your unhealthy habits, here are some steps you can take to eliminate them more quickly and thoroughly:

Set a goal. Set a goal for yourself and plan how you will achieve it. If you want to reduce the amount of time you spend on social media, look for an option on your phone that places an allotted time limit for specific apps to help you follow through. Choosing a different fun activity to do after you reach your time limit for the day can help make the habit stick. If you normally scroll social media for an hour and you decrease that to 30 minutes a day, use that other 30 minutes on a hobby you enjoy. Changing this reward each day can keep things exciting throughout the process.

Replace unhealthy habits with healthy ones. Another way to call it quits on a bad habit is to find a better alternative. For instance, if you snack on junk food in the afternoon, choose some healthy foods you really enjoy to help change the habit. Making a list of alternatives will help you follow through with breaking the habit.

Create a supportive environment. Surround yourself with people who support your efforts to eliminate unhealthy habits. You can also seek resources such as support groups or counseling if you need additional help.

Deal with your triggers. Almost everything in life follows a pattern of cause and effect. There is no tree without a seed. Once you've identified your unhealthy habits, it's essential to understand what triggers them and try to tackle those underlying causes instead. For example, if you eat junk food when stressed, finding other ways to cope with stress, such as exercise or meditation, can help you break the habit.

Be patient. Breaking free from unhealthy habits takes time and patience. Don't expect to change overnight, and don't get discouraged if you slip up. Simply pick yourself up and try again. Remember that every small step you take is still progress.

Creating a Daily Routine That Promotes Healthy Habits

A daily routine promoting healthy habits is critical to a healthy lifestyle. We've already discussed creating routines and schedules, but here are some more tips regarding building healthy habits into your life:

Start your day with a healthy habit. Incorporate a healthy habit such as drinking a glass of water or doing a quick yoga session into your morning routine.

Make healthy choices easy. Keep healthy snacks on hand, pack your gym bag the night before, and plan your meals. By taking time the night before to prepare as much as you can, you decrease the number of decisions you need to make in the morning.

Find a workout you enjoy. Exercise doesn't have to be tedious or painful! Make a list of all the physical activities you enjoy (e.g., dancing, playing outside games with friends, bike riding, yoga) and vary what you do each day.

Take breaks throughout the day. Taking breaks throughout the day can help you stay focused and energized. Use your breaks to stretch, take a short walk, or meditate. Some people enjoy doodling or journaling as well.

Wind down at night. Establish a nighttime routine that helps you wind down and prepare for sleep. This might include reading a book, taking a warm bath, or light stretching. It's a good idea to turn off electronics an hour before sleep and keep a consistent bedtime for the best results.

ACTIVITY: TRYING A NEW HEALTHY RECIPE

Trying a new healthy recipe is a great way to build healthy eating habits. You can improve your health and well-being by incorporating new nutritious foods into your diet. Here's an activity to help you get started:

- **Find a healthy recipe:** These can be found online or by flipping through your family's recipe books. You can also ask your friends or the adults in your life for their favorite healthy recipes.
- **Shop for ingredients:** Once you've found a recipe you want to try, list the ingredients you'll need. Go to the grocery store or farmers market and gather the necessary

ingredients. It is a good idea to choose a recipe that uses spices you already have available; otherwise, new recipes can get quite expensive.

- **Prepare the recipe:** Follow the recipe's instructions and prepare your healthy meal. If you're new to cooking, start with something simple like a salad or stir-fry. If you're experienced, challenge yourself with a more complex recipe.

- **Enjoy your meal:** Sit down and savor your healthy meal. Pay attention to the flavors and textures of the food and how it makes you feel. Take note of any adjustments you might want to make for next time.

Trying new, healthy recipes is a fun and rewarding way to help build healthy eating habits. Cooking for others is also a nice way to let them know you appreciate them!

CHAPTER FOUR:
MANAGING STRESS
AND ANXIETY

Stress and anxiety are two recurrent and interconnected emotional states that can adversely affect your mental and physical health. Stress is a normal physiological reaction to a perceived threat or challenge, whether actual or imagined, and it isn't just in your head. It can also cause physical reactions such as increased heart rate and blood pressure. Stress can be acute, such as in response to an unanticipated event that prompts a fight-or-flight response, or chronic.

On the other hand, anxiety is a state of discomfort or fear that can result from a range of actual or perceived situations or stimuli. It's a natural reaction to stressful or complex conditions, but it can interfere with your daily activities if it becomes chronic and overpowering.

You might have experienced some of the symptoms of stress and anxiety without even knowing it. Some physical effects of stress and anxiety are headache, fatigue, stomachache, and muscle tension. In some cases, chronic stress can lead to long-term health problems such as cardiovascular disease.

The effects of stress and anxiety aren't limited to the physical aspects alone. Stress and anxiety can cause a range of emotional symptoms as well. You may become irritable, moody, or easily agitated. You may also experience feelings of sadness, hopelessness, or helplessness. In severe cases, stress and anxiety can lead to depression, which can have serious consequences if left untreated.

Social stress and anxiety can also affect your relationships with peers and family members. You may become withdrawn, avoid social activities, or have difficulty communicating. Anxiety can also cause you to develop social phobias or bring on panic attacks, making it challenging to participate in activities that you once enjoyed. At school, stress and anxiety can negatively impact your academic performance; you may struggle to concentrate, have difficulty completing assignments, or experience test anxiety. Chronic stress can also lead to burnout, causing you to lose motivation and interest in your studies.

There are several ways to get help and manage stress and anxiety if you already have any of these symptoms. Physical activity such as sports or yoga can encourage relaxation and reduce stress. In just a bit, we'll discuss some techniques like deep breathing that can manage the symptoms of stress and anxiety. Consulting a mental health specialist for professional assistance can also provide you with strategies to manage those symptoms and address the underlying issues that may be causing them.

CALMING TECHNIQUES

There are several techniques that can be effective in managing stress and anxiety, including the following:

Deep breathing: Deep breathing can help relax your nervous system. When you're stressed, your breathing may become quick and shallow. To practice deep breathing, find a quiet space to relax, then close your eyes and concentrate on your breathing. Inhale deeply through your nose while counting to four. Try to fill your entire stomach and chest with air. Hold your breath for a count of four. Exhale through your mouth for a count of four. Repeating this while counting will help refocus your mind onto your body while delivering oxygen to your system. Try to continue this cycle of four-count breaths for at least two minutes.

Meditation: Meditation has been practiced for thousands of years and comes in many different forms. By focusing the mind on a specific object or mantra, meditation can quiet mental chatter and bring your body back into a relaxed state. There are many short guided meditations available online, which can be helpful when you first start out. However, you don't really need anything to begin. One easy meditation technique is to sit outside. If possible, put your bare feet on the ground by sitting on a porch step or lawn chair. Otherwise, any comfortable position is okay. Close your eyes, place your palms down flat on your thighs, and start taking deep breaths. As you're breathing, count and focus on five places where you can feel your body. For example, you might pay attention to the feeling of your hands on your thighs, where your feet touch the ground, how your heartbeat feels, the air on your skin, or the way your body sits on your porch or seat. You can also do this with sounds or smells. The important thing is to focus your attention on something specific outside of your thoughts to ground you.

Another easy meditation technique is the practice of "emptiness." Many people struggle with this at first, often finding it difficult to stay focused when they start out. That's perfectly normal! The goal isn't to be good at it but to keep trying. To practice, get into a comfortable position, either sitting or lying down. Close your eyes and focus on your breath moving through your body. As thoughts and worries come into your mind, imagine each one as a balloon. Observe the thought, then let it go. Each time a new thought comes into your mind, release it and return your focus to your breath. You might find you have to refocus every few seconds. This is okay, so don't worry about it; it's part of the process. The goal is to keep releasing thoughts and refocusing on your breath each time you notice you've become distracted.

Exercise: Regular physical activity is an effective technique for managing stress and anxiety. During exercise, your body releases endorphins, which are naturally occurring mood enhancers that aid in stress reduction and promote a sense of well-being. Exercise can also reduce muscle tension and improve sleep quality, which is vital for managing stress. Even just a short walk or gentle stretching can be beneficial. Still, moderate to vigorous physical activity for at least one hour most days of the week is recommended for the best results. If you can't do an hour, that's okay! Every little bit helps. You also don't have to complete the whole hour at once; doing short 10 to 15 minute sets of exercise throughout the day is just as helpful as a whole hour all at once.

Progressive muscle relaxation: Progressive muscle relaxation involves tensing and relaxing various muscle groups in your body one at a time. This technique helps to release tension from the body. To practice progressive muscle relaxation, find a quiet space to lie comfortably and close your eyes. Starting with your feet, tense the muscles in that area for a few seconds before releasing the tension and relaxing. Move slowly up the body, tensing and relaxing each muscle group, including the legs, stomach, chest, arms, hands, and face. As you release tension from each muscle group, focus on the sensation of relaxation and allow yourself to sink deeper into a state of calm.

Mindfulness: Mindfulness involves focusing on the current moment without distraction or judgment. By focusing on the present moment, you become more aware of your thoughts, emotions, and any physical sensations you're experiencing, which will allow you to manage them more effectively. There are numerous ways to develop mindfulness, including meditation, yoga, and breathing exercises. You can practice mindfulness on a daily basis by paying attention to your surroundings, thoughts, emotions, and interactions with your friends and peers. According to research, frequently practicing mindfulness lowers symptoms of anxiety and depression and improves sleep quality. One exercise that may help is to make a mental list observing your senses. What do you hear, smell, feel, and taste? Be specific, and try to list as many observations as possible. This is especially helpful to combine with breathing techniques.

Social support: Social support means seeking out and relying on the support of others. A strong network of friends, family, and other supportive individuals can provide a sense of belonging and connection that can be invaluable when facing stress and anxiety. Social support can take many forms, including talking to a friend or loved one, joining a support group, or seeking professional counseling. Research has shown that individuals with strong social support networks tend to have better mental and physical health outcomes, including lower stress and anxiety levels. If you struggle to find a sense of belonging, there are often options to make friends within your community. Local game stores, cafés, libraries, community centers, and online groups often carry information on upcoming events. Online communities are a great way to meet with people with the same interests; however, it's extremely important to keep yourself safe. Strangers are still strangers even if they're online and should be approached with the same level of caution as meeting new people in person. It's easy to create fake profiles and conceal real identities online. Talk to your guardian about safety precautions, ground rules, and warning signs before joining online communities.

Change your surroundings: Sometimes, when you're overwhelmed, a simple change of scenery can help you mentally reset. Taking a short walk, running an errand, making a phone call to a friend, or completing a chore outside of your normal routine can help you to focus on something other than what's bothering you. If you're at school, request a short bathroom break to practice breathing or meditation for a minute. If you're at work, stepping outside for five minutes and soaking up some sunshine can help you relax.

It's important to try as many different approaches to stress management as you need to figure out what works best for you. You may find that you use a different technique for each unique situation. Remember that whatever is going on right now is sure to change. No matter how grim a situation feels in the moment, it will usually pass in time.

SELF-CARE AND RELAXATION

Self-care and relaxation are important practices for anyone who wants to stay balanced despite life's stressors. By taking time for yourself and engaging in activities that promote relaxation and well-being, you can reduce your stress level, improve your mood, sleep better, and give your brain a boost. Here are some ideas to help you take care of yourself:

Self-Care:
- Take a bath
- Spend extra time grooming
- Complete a deep organization project
- Finish a task you've procrastinated on due to lack of time
- Go for a walk
- Spend time with friends and family
- Plan something special for the weekend
- Attend a play or movie

Relaxation:
- Watch a movie
- Complete an art project
- Meditate
- Spend time with your pet or animals
- Engage in anything that makes you laugh
- Sunbathe
- Drink your favorite beverage outside
- Listen to music
- Journal
- Read a book
- Dance

ACTIVITY: PRACTICE MINDFULNESS AND MEDITATION

- Find a comfortable place to sit, either on the floor or in a chair. Keep your back straight and relax your shoulders.

- Close your eyes and take a few deep breaths, inhaling through your nose and exhaling through your mouth.

- Concentrate on your breathing. Take note of how your breath feels as it enters and exits your body. Don't try to change or control your breath; just observe it.

- As you continue to focus on your breath, notice any thoughts or feelings that arise. Acknowledge them, but avoid getting caught up in them. Just observe them and let them go.

- Now, imagine yourself in a peaceful place. This could be a beach, a forest, a meadow, or anywhere else that feels calm and relaxing. Use your senses to bring this place to life. What do you see, hear, smell, and feel?

- As you continue to visualize this peaceful place, think of someone or something that you're grateful for. It could be a friend, a family member, a pet, or anything else that brings you joy. Take a moment to appreciate this person or thing and feel grateful.

- Bring your attention back to your breath. Take a few deep breaths through your nose and out through your mouth.

- Open your eyes when you're ready and focus on the present.

This guided meditation exercise can be customized to meet your specific needs. You can modify the exact steps to suit your needs. Regular practice will help you achieve mindfulness and inner calm.

CHAPTER FIVE: BUILDING SELF-CONFIDENCE

Feeling uncertain or insecure about yourself and your abilities is common as a teenager. You might feel pressure to fit in with your peers or worry that you're "not good enough" in some way. However, building self-confidence is essential to growing up to become a happy, healthy adult. Self-confidence allows you to trust yourself, believe in your abilities, and feel comfortable in your skin.

This chapter will explore strategies for building self-confidence as a teenager. These strategies have been tested over the years and can help you develop a positive self-image, overcome self-doubt, and feel more comfortable expressing yourself. With practice and persistence, you can become a more confident, self-assured person who's ready to take on the challenges of adulthood.

THE IMPORTANCE OF SELF-CONFIDENCE

Self-confidence is an essential aspect of mental health and well-being. It's that feel-good part of yourself that helps you trust your decisions and take on new challenges positively. When you have self-confidence, you're less likely to be held back by self-doubt or negative self-talk and more likely to take risks and pursue your goals. Self-confidence allows you to feel ready for the experiences that life has to offer as you go through its stages. Here are some key reasons why self-confidence is so important:

Delivering your best effort when it matters. According to research, people are more likely to do their best when they're confident. Those who experience self-doubt will downplay their strengths, which can hinder their pursuits to become creatives, thought leaders, actors, musicians, and athletes. Having confidence enables you to perform at your best when under pressure. It doesn't end there; your confidence can help your peers too! You can influence or inspire other people just by doing things confidently.

Possessing personal power. Inner strength is strongly related to increased self-confidence. Your ability to think, act, speak, and carry yourself with confidence grows over time. The more you can hold your own, the more control you will develop over every part of your life. When you control your confidence, you become more empowered and positive. The confidence that you develop for yourself can help you focus on the bigger picture about who you are, regardless of bad days and setbacks.

Feeling worthy and valued. When you're self-confident, you know your capabilities, advantages, and how you may benefit those around you. What you get in return is the appreciation of people that you have been able to positively impact. You feel valuable and useful because you know you have what it takes to succeed.

Reducing damaging thoughts. Freedom from self-doubt and negative or destructive thinking increases with greater self-confidence. Being confident in yourself makes you feel less anxious and more courageous. Your willingness and determination to venture beyond your comfort zone and take calculated risks will build your self-confidence. Ultimately, self-confidence improves your mental health by allowing you to cultivate a positive self-image. This can also reduce symptoms of depression, anxiety, and other mental health issues.

Preventing social anxiety. When you focus on yourself, you don't dwell about what others think about you. Understanding that you're just as valuable as everyone else can soothe the normal fears that pop up during social interactions. Even if a social interaction doesn't go well, knowing your worth enables you to cope with temporary feelings of rejection.

Improving relationships: Self-confidence can also help you build better relationships with others. Feeling good about yourself makes you more likely to be assertive, communicate effectively, and establish healthy boundaries.

Experiencing increased resilience. Self-confidence can help you bounce back from setbacks and challenges. When you strongly believe in yourself and your abilities, you're less likely to be discouraged by failure or criticism.

HOW TO BUILD SELF-CONFIDENCE

Here are some methods to help you increase your self-assurance and boost your self-confidence:

Positive affirmations: Positive self-affirmation is a powerful tool for building self-confidence and self-esteem. It involves regularly repeating positive statements to yourself, which can help you replace negative thought habits with constructive ones. Positive self-affirmations allow you to feel more confident, capable, and worthy. Use positive affirmations to build your confidence. Repeat positive affirmations such as "I am capable," "I am worthy," and "I can do this" to yourself. Positive self-affirmations train your subconscious mind to concentrate on your abilities and the good things in your life. This helps you develop a more positive outlook, leading to improved mental and physical health. Positive self-affirmation can be practiced in many ways such as repeating positive statements to yourself in the mirror, writing positive affirmations on sticky notes and placing them in visible places, or reciting positive affirmations at the start of your day and before going to bed.

Small goals: Although it's good to have long-term goals, when your confidence feels a little low, it helps to scale everything back until you feel stronger. Setting small tasks and accomplishing them increases self-efficacy, which is basically your belief in your own abilities. Completing a to-do list of simple tasks such as drinking a glass of water when waking up, brushing your teeth, and sitting in the sun for 10 minutes will help you feel better. You can increase the difficulty of your tasks as you feel more confident in your ability to complete them.

Personal strengths: Embracing your strengths is a powerful way to build self-confidence and self-esteem. Everyone has special abilities and strengths; discover what you're good at and concentrate on enhancing those strengths. This involves accepting and valuing yourself for what you can do and who you are. To embrace your strengths, take stock of your abilities and identify areas in which you excel. Consider whether you have a particular skill or talent, a special personality trait, or even a set of unique values that guide your actions. Once you've identified your strengths, find ways to develop and hone those skills. You can take classes, attend workshops, or seek out mentors who can help you grow and learn.

Learning new skills: Learning new skills is an excellent way to boost self-confidence and self-esteem. When you learn a new skill, you're expanding your knowledge and abilities, which can help you feel more competent. Learning new skills can also help you step out of your comfort zone as you overcome self-doubt and fear. One approach to choosing the right skill to learn is thinking of someone or something you admire. If you think juggling is really cool or admire someone who is extremely organized, you might want to work toward developing those skills. Remember that you probably won't be good at something new when you first start. That's a normal part of the process! However, developing the skills you admire in other people will lead to you feeling better about yourself in the long run.

Surrounding yourself with the right people: It's important to remember that not every person is the right fit for your ambitions, sense of humor, or personality. This is normal. Surrounding yourself with good people who truly appreciate you for who you are will help you remember the good aspects about your personality. If being around a certain group of friends leaves you feeling self-conscious or drained, they're probably not the people you should spend your free time with. Making new friends can be difficult, but you can find them by seeking out clubs and communities centered around your interests. Even within your family, try spending more time with people who leave you feeling the best and most accepted.

DEALING WITH SELF-DOUBT AND NEGATIVE SELF-TALK

Self-doubt and negative self-talk tend to grow if left unchecked. Although it's normal to have moments when you don't feel or think positive things about yourself, there are strategies that can help you refocus. Nobody's perfect, but practicing positive thinking can help you appreciate the best aspects of yourself. Here are some strategies to deal with self-doubt and negative self-talk:

Identify negative self-talk. Recognizing negative language is a valuable strategy to enhance your mental and emotional well-being. Self-criticism, self-doubt, and unpleasant comments are all examples of negative talk. Using phrases like "always" and "never" are usually a good indication of negative thoughts. For example, you may think *I never win anything* or *I always mess things up.* These statements are rarely true, and you can counteract them by focusing your attention on why they're inaccurate.

Challenge negative thoughts. This is a skill you should practice every day. Once you've discovered a negative idea, question it by asking yourself if it's true and if there's evidence to back it up. You can also try to reframe the concept by making it more positive or realistic. Instead of thinking that you'll never be successful, reframe it as *I'm not perfect, but I am making progress, and that's what matters.* You can also focus on gratitude. If you think something bad about your appearance, instead of indulging in that thought, make a list of the things you *do* like. Maybe you don't like your nose, but you really like the color of your eyes. Concentrate on the parts of yourself that you're grateful for. Another method to challenge negative thoughts is utilizing positive affirmations or visualization techniques. Using these tactics regularly will retrain your brain to think more positively and empower you to develop a more resilient attitude.

Practice self-compassion. Self-compassion involves being just as nice, considerate, and understanding to yourself as you would to someone else. Start by identifying your problems and accepting that making errors or experiencing tough emotions is a normal part of the life. You should have the same empathy and compassion for yourself that you would extend to someone you love. Next time you think something negative, ask yourself if you'd say that out loud to one of your friends. When something doesn't go your way, ask yourself what advice or encouragement you would give to a loved one in the same situation.

Surround yourself with positivity. Being surrounded by a positive environment can significantly impact your life for the better. As a teenager, you can't control every aspect of your environment. Although this can be frustrating, you can increase the positivity around you by focusing on the areas you *do* control. Negative individuals and circumstances will sap your energy, increase stress, and make it harder to maintain a happy attitude. Begin by building positive relationships with friends, family, and peers who support and encourage you. Look for people who share your ideals and motivate you to be your best. You can also create a pleasant environment by surrounding yourself with things that make you happy, such as meaningful artwork or music, plants, and items that remind you of pleasant memories. When possible, try to consume positive material such as uplifting books, movies, or podcasts, and limit exposure to negative news or social media.

Focus on the present moment. This mindfulness technique enables you to overcome self-doubt and negative self-talk and concentrate on the present. By focusing on the here and now, you let go of your fears about the past or the future. Be sure to use all your senses, taking in the sights, sounds, smells, and sensations around you. Engage fully in whatever you are doing and try to bring a sense of curiosity and openness to the experience. You can develop a more optimistic mindset and handle self-doubt and negative self-talk by implementing these ideas.

ACTIVITY: WRITE DOWN POSITIVE AFFIRMATIONS

You can use the positive affirmations below to deal with self-doubt and negative self-talk. Write them out on a paper or poster and paste them in areas that you'll see throughout the day. Recite them to yourself every morning before you leave the house and before going to bed each night.

I am capable and strong.

I am worthy of love and respect.

I deserve happiness and success.

I believe in myself and my abilities.

I believe in the choices and decisions I make.

I am grateful for all the good in my life.

I am unique and special.

I stand out in the path that the universe has set for me.

I am surrounded by positive energy and love.

I am enough, just as I am.

It's a good idea to write some of your own personalized affirmations as well. Consider possible affirmations throughout your daily life and add to the list whenever you think of a new one.

CHAPTER SIX: MAKING GOOD DECISIONS

A good decision is founded on a thorough understanding of the situation, its potential outcomes, and the implications of each option. It's best to employ a logical and systematic technique that involves critical thinking, problem solving, and weighing many choices. Good decision-making entails paying attention to the advantages and disadvantages of each option, calculating the risks and benefits, and considering the effects they will have on yourself and others. It also necessitates the ability to foresee unfavorable outcomes and adapt to changing conditions. Good decision-making is a skill that can be learned and improved upon over time, and it's essential for personal, professional, and social success.

HOW TO MAKE
GOOD DECISIONS

People have tried various techniques to improve their decision-making abilities over the years; some have proven to be effective for everyone, while others only work for some people. This section touches on some of the most commonly used approaches to decision-making.

To begin with, it's crucial to define the problem before making any decisions. This helps you understand the root of an issue and frame the decision in the right context. Oftentimes, this is best done after taking a step back from the issue. Whenever possible, try to get a good night's sleep and get some mental distance before tackling an issue.

Once you've rested and spent some time away from the problem, analyze it from all angles. Think about what the underlying causes are and what potential consequences are involved. For example, if your friend asks you to a party past your curfew, a possible consequence is that you could end up grounded or otherwise punished. You should also list out why you want to go to the party, what you expect to experience from the party, and if your expectations are realistic.

Gathering information is important to understanding your decision in the right context. For a party, you'll want to ask who will be present, if there will be supervision, and if there are any illegal activities planned. Knowing what to expect before accepting or declining will help you understand whether it's a safe choice or not. If the problem has to do with something like choosing the right school or scholarship to apply for, you'll want to conduct more in-depth research, which may benefit from the help of mentors, the library, or online databases.

Once you've gathered information, it's critical to explore all your viable options by considering alternatives. This could include brainstorming, mind mapping, or another creative technique. Consider your alternatives by producing various prospective solutions or choices and weighing their benefits against the drawbacks. When you're finished, select the one that best matches your values and goals. If you want to attend the party, an alternative solution to breaking curfew may be to ask if you can stay out late as a one-time exception.

Making a good decision entails selecting the best course of action based on the information at hand. It's important to clearly choose one way forward. Although some things will naturally work themselves out, oftentimes *not* making a choice can be just as harmful as making the wrong choice. This is especially true when it comes to opportunities, communication within your relationships, and prioritizing the tasks in your daily life. It's healthy to have flexibility in your life, but allowing the majority of your choices to be made by happenstance will end with outside forces determining how your life turns out.

Once you take action, evaluate the results to determine whether the choice was effective. This can help you identify areas for improvement and make more informed decisions in the future. Compare your expected results to the actual results, taking note of where things went wrong and recording anything that you didn't foresee while making your original decision.

THINKING LONG TERM

Thinking long term means planning and considering the potential outcomes of your decisions and actions over a significant period of time. It involves taking a strategic approach to decision-making, anticipating potential risks, investing in relationships, and prioritizing responsibility. In this fast-paced world, getting caught up in the moment and losing sight of the big picture is easy. However, by thinking about the future, you'll be able to set yourself up for success and growth.

One of the most significant benefits of thinking long term is the ability to engage in strategic planning. When you think over an extended period, you can develop strategies that are aligned with your goals. For example, if you're planning to start a business, thinking long term means considering potential challenges and opportunities that may arise in the future. This can help you allocate resources in the most effective way possible and position yourself for future success.

Another benefit of thinking long term is risk management. You'll be better prepared to handle unexpected setbacks by anticipating potential risks and challenges. If you're saving money for a down payment on a car, thinking long term means considering the potential for job loss or unexpected expenses that may affect your ability to save. By planning for these scenarios, you can mitigate potential risks and ensure that you're well prepared to handle any challenges that come your way.

Thinking long term also allows you to grow. Investing in research and development and pursuing innovative solutions can position you for future success. If you're preparing for college, thinking long term means considering potential career paths and opportunities to stand out on your applications. This can help you identify areas where you can develop new skills and gain experience.

Another important benefit of thinking long term is building relationships. By investing in your relationships with your friends and peers, you can build solid and lasting connections that can help you succeed in the future. For example, thinking long term might mean fostering loyalty and trust among members of a team or organization. This can help you work together more effectively and achieve greater success in the future.

Finally, thinking long term means prioritizing sustainability and environmental responsibility. By considering the long-term impact of your actions, you can ensure that you use resources responsibly and appropriately. If you're thinking about purchasing a car, thinking long term means considering the environmental impact of your purchase and choosing a vehicle that's fuel efficient or environmentally friendly.

As you can see, thinking long term is an essential skill that can help you achieve sustainable success and ensure future growth. By developing your ability to think long term, you'll be better prepared to handle unexpected events, position yourself for future success, and build lasting connections with those around you.

ACTIVITY: DECISION-MAKING GAME

- **Identify a decision you need to make:** Before you can begin weighing the pros and cons of different options, you need to be clear about what decisions you're facing. This might involve brainstorming a list of decisions and then narrowing it down to the ones that are most important or time sensitive.
- **Get a clean piece of paper:** Having a dedicated space to map out your decision-making process can keep your thoughts organized and focused. A blank piece of paper provides a fresh start and a visual representation of your decision-making process.

- **Draw a line down the center of your paper:** This step involves dividing the paper into two distinct sections. The left side will be for listing the positive aspects of a potential solution, while the right side will focus on the negative aspects.

- **On the left side, write out positives:** List out all the benefits of choosing a particular path. These advantages might include increased financial gain, improved health and wellness, or greater personal fulfillment.

- **On the right side, write out negatives:** Next, it's time to consider the downsides of deciding on a certain solution to your problem. This might include potential risks or challenges such as financial costs, time constraints, or negative impacts on your relationships or well-being.

- **Assign a weight to each positive or negative based on how important it is to you:** Not all pros and cons are created equal, so it's important to consider which factors are most significant to you. If financial stability is a top priority, you might assign a higher weight to any potential financial benefits or drawbacks.

- **Total the weights for each side to see which is more compelling:** Once you've assigned weights to each factor, it's time to add them up to determine which path has the most overall appeal. If one side of the paper has a much higher total weight than the other, that might indicate a clear winner. However, if the two sides are relatively evenly matched, you may need additional reflection or research before making a final decision.

- **Reflect on the results and make your decision:** After you've completed the previous steps, take some time to reflect on what you've learned. Consider how the pros and cons align with your values, priorities, and goals. Use this information to inform your final decision; trust your instincts and act accordingly.

CHAPTER SEVEN: DEVELOPING STRONG RELATIONSHIPS

As a teen, you're going through a period of change in which you'll discover new things about yourself and the world around you every day. Creating connections with people is an important part of this journey. Building solid relationships is essential to living a happy and full life, whether they be with family, friends, or romantic partners.

As you read on, you will learn various advantages of building solid relationships as well as some advice and methods for doing so. Communication skills and conflict-resolution strategies are also important for building long-lasting, secure relationships.

THE IMPORTANCE OF HEALTHY RELATIONSHIPS

As you navigate the ups and downs of life, your well-being will be closely linked to the quality of your relationships with peers, family, and mentors. Healthy relationships provide a sense of belonging, support, and positive reinforcement, which can bolster self-esteem and emotional resilience. On the other hand, aspects of negative relationships, such as bullying or conflict with family members, can lead to anxiety, depression, and other mental health issues. Teenagers who lack positive social connections may also be more susceptible to risky behaviors such as substance abuse or self-harm. Therefore, building and maintaining solid and healthy relationships is crucial for your overall well-being and long-term success.

What is a Healthy Relationship?

A relationship is healthy when both people feel heard, respected, and valued. A healthy connection is one in which you feel free to be who you are, say what's on your mind, and collaborate to find solutions to issues. Compromise, effort, and communication are necessary components of a healthy partnership on both sides. When a relationship is healthy, interactions will leave you feeling good afterwards. It's normal to have conflict from time to time, but you shouldn't experience arguments or bad feelings on a regular basis.

Negative Impacts of Unhealthy Relationships

Being in a toxic or abusive relationship can have an impact on your self-worth and happiness, resulting in low moods, anxiety, and even depression. Here are some concrete ways that unhealthy relationships might harm you:

Emotional and mental health: Unhealthy relationships can produce negative emotions such as anxiety, despair, low self-esteem, and hopelessness. They could also result in you believing and accepting that you are not deserving of respect and kindness or that you're simply not good enough.

Physical well-being: Negative relationships also have an effect on your physical health. Physical symptoms such as headaches, stomachaches, and difficulty sleeping can be caused by stress, anxiety, and other negative emotions. In addition to these symptoms, crying or fighting could cause you to lose sleep or hamper your ability to focus throughout the day.

Academic and social life: Being in an unhealthy relationship can also have an impact on these spheres of your daily life. You may become distracted from your studies and do poorly in class as a result. Additionally, you might start to notice a decline in your social life in general if you've had bad experiences with a few peers.

Future connections: Being involved in unhealthy relationships can affect your ability to recognize healthy ones in the future. You could find it difficult to understand what healthy relationships look like if you're used to being in toxic ones.

BUILDING STRONG RELATIONSHIPS

Building solid, healthy relationships requires effective communication between or among every party involved. It entails speaking the truth, participating in conversations, and respectfully expressing your emotions. It also requires that you make an effort to stay in touch with the good people in your life on a regular basis and be receptive to their opinions as well.

Furthermore, building effective relationships requires setting boundaries. In relationships, boundaries are the upper and lower limitations that you set for yourself regarding what you're willing to do for others and what you are comfortable having them do for you. Setting and upholding boundaries keeps your self-worth intact and guards you against being abused or mistreated. Reflect on your levels of comfort and discomfort with various aspects of your relationships. This may include the length of time you're willing to spend with someone, the kind of physical contact you're comfortable with, or the types of discussions you want to have with others.

The following are ways to build strong and healthy relationships:

Empathy: This is the ability to place yourself in another person's position and attempt to comprehend their viewpoint. This can facilitate deeper interactions with others and a greater comprehension of their wants and needs.

Respect: Treating people with respect is acting in a way that you would like to be treated. It entails accepting and honoring their opinions, emotions, limits, needs, and preferences.

Trust: A healthy relationship requires trust in order to function. To build trust, you must be honest, sincere, and open with the people in your life. Make an effort to fulfill your obligations, maintain your word, and take responsibility for your deeds.

Quality time: Spending quality time with the people in your life may strengthen your bonds and help you make memories that will last a lifetime. Try to plan frequent time with your family, friends, and romantic partners. When you spend time together, concentrate on being present and involved.

Compromise: Finding a mutually beneficial middle ground is the essence of compromise. Compromise means being open to hearing many points of view and collaborating to develop win-win solutions without thinking your wants are more important.

Forgiveness: Since no relationship is perfect, there will undoubtedly be times when someone disappoints or offends you. Forgiveness is the ability to set aside rage and bitterness while working to mend the relationship.

Resolving Conflicts in Your Relationships

You will inevitably experience conflict even in the healthiest of relationships; thus, developing good conflict-resolution skills is essential. The following are some suggestions for handling disagreements in your relationships:

Understand the problem: Clarifying the subject at hand is the first step in settling a dispute. This might require sitting down and reflecting on your wants and feelings or speaking with the other person to understand their point of view.

Actively listen: After determining the problem, pay attention to what the other person has to say. This means that you must be open to hearing them out without interrupting or becoming hostile. Make an effort to understand their perspective completely.

Express your wants and feelings: After hearing the other person out, it's important to respectfully and clearly state your needs and desires. Focus on expressing your own feelings rather than accusing or criticizing the other person.

Come up with a solution together: After both of you have had a chance to voice your wants and feelings, come up with a solution that works for both of you. This may involve making concessions or developing a novel solution that satisfies both your needs.

Follow up: After the conflict has been addressed, it's important to check in to see if the solution you came up with is still working for both of you. To do this, you need to check in with the other person involved and make necessary adjustments till the issue is completely resolved.

ELIMINATING TOXIC RELATIONSHIPS

In addition to fostering healthy connections, it's essential to identify and get rid of toxic ones. Your mental and emotional health may suffer from toxic relationships, which may also have an adverse effect on other aspects of your life. The following are some pointers for spotting and ending unhealthy relationships:

Recognize the symptoms: Constant criticism or negativity, a lack of empathy or support, manipulative behavior, and a history of abusing your trust are typical indicators of a toxic relationship.

Trust your gut: If something about a relationship seems odd, trust your gut. Feelings of anxiety or apprehension around someone may indicate a toxic relationship with that person. Another indication is that they frequently make you feel negatively about yourself.

Establish limits: Protecting yourself requires establishing firm boundaries in any relationship. Be upfront and respectful when expressing your demands and desires. It could be time to reconsider the relationship if someone repeatedly tests your boundaries or makes you feel uncomfortable.

Speak with a professional: If you need support or you're involved in a toxic relationship, don't hesitate to seek out a mental health professional or guidance counselor. They may offer you insight and direction and assist you in creating a strategy for dealing with the situation.

Let go: In some instances, ending a toxic relationship is the best thing you can do for your health. This could be challenging, especially if you've put a lot of time and effort into the relationship, but in the end, it's essential to put your well-being first. One way you can make this easier is by distancing yourself from the other person. You can do this by limiting contact—in person and online—while you decide on the best course of action.

Remember that it's perfectly acceptable to end relationships that aren't helping you or are causing you harm. You can build a life full of healthy, fulfilling relationships by being aware of the telltale indications of an unhealthy relationship, establishing appropriate boundaries, asking for help, and letting go when required.

ACTIVITY: WRITING A LETTER

An essential strategy to create and maintain solid connections is expressing gratitude. Writing a letter is a quick and effective way to show appreciation to someone else. It enables you to thoughtfully and meaningfully communicate your emotions while letting the other person know how much they matter to you.

Start by thinking of a person who has positively influenced you. It might be someone from your family, a friend, a mentor, or a teacher. Consider what they have done for you and the reasons you value them. This will enable you to write a more emotional and personal letter.

Write the person's name in the beginning and explain the purpose of the letter: *Dear [Name], I just wanted to take a moment to show my gratitude for everything you've done for me.*

Elaborate on how this person has improved your life in specific ways. Use examples to support your views, and be as honest as you can. *I'll never forget the time when you [specific action or event]. I appreciate your generosity and assistance; you've made a big difference in my life.* Alternatively, you may say: *Your advice and encouragement helped me [specific success or goal]. Without you, I wouldn't have been able to do it, and I appreciate you believing in me so much.*

Finally, thank the person again and tell them how much they mean to you in your letter's closing. You may finish by saying: *Thank you once more for everything you do. You are a genuinely wonderful person, and I am truly grateful to have you in my life.*

Remember that sending a letter can help you understand your own feelings about your relationships and strengthen your connections with others. Write a letter to someone you appreciate today and see how it improves your relationships with those around you.

CHAPTER EIGHT:
MANAGING MONEY

As a teenager, your access to money may be limited. With that said, there are still ways you can build good financial habits and set long-term goals that will greatly benefit your future. Whether you're saving from an allowance, birthday gifts, or a part-time job, there's always room to start thinking about ways to improve your financial health as soon as possible.

Unless you've been living under a rock your whole life, you know that money is a medium of exchange that enables you to buy goods and services. It takes many different forms, such as cash, credit cards, and digital currencies. Managing money can be a daunting task for anyone regardless of age. It's always tempting to spend money on *everything*, particularly the things that seem to be trending, such as the latest gadget or fashion. It is, however, vital that you learn the skill of proper money management. This essential skill may not seem important to you now, but it will be of great use as you grow older. In this chapter, you'll learn strategies to effectively manage money, avoid debt, and build a strong financial foundation for your future.

FINANCIAL RESPONSIBILITY

Financial responsibility is the ability to handle your finances in a prudent way. It requires that you make wise decisions on how you earn, save, spend, and invest your money while also avoiding excessive debt and financial risks. Financial responsibility includes making a budget and sticking to it, saving for emergencies and future goals, paying bills on time, avoiding unnecessary expenses, and making informed choices about investments.

You shouldn't invest in something without doing your own research. Being financially responsible requires you to understand the potential risks and rewards associated with different financial decisions. It means taking steps to protect yourself from financial fraud and scams and seeking professional advice when needed. You have to take ownership of your financial well-being and make choices that support your long-term financial stability.

Saving money is another vital aspect of being financially responsible. You should always set aside a percentage of your paycheck to develop an emergency fund that can be used to pay for unforeseen needs without having to borrow money.

While many people see the use of credit cards as a timely escape route to financial challenges, it's important that you understand the risks of using one. No doubt, credit cards are convenient, but if you're not careful, they can lead to unmanageable debt. You should avoid credit cards unless you completely understand how they function and you can pay off the balance *in full* each month.

Learning these skills as a teenager will help you reach financial independence. This means having enough money to support yourself without help from others. You can learn to live within your means and make wise financial decisions by developing a budget, conserving money, and avoiding debt. Being financially responsible will also teach you the value of hard work and the significance of earning and saving money.

MANAGING MONEY EFFECTIVELY

Effective money management is a valuable life skill that can help you achieve your financial objectives and safeguard your financial future. Here are some methods for managing your money effectively:

Create a budget: A budget is a plan that assists in categorizing your expenses, savings, and investments. It's an excellent tool for successful money management because it allows you to keep track of where your money is going and discover areas where you may need to cut back.

Automate your savings: Saving automatically is a terrific method of developing healthy financial habits and attaining long-term financial objectives. You can save money without even thinking about it if you set up a monthly automatic transfer from your checking account to your savings account. Automating your savings is simple and handy, and it can help you avoid spending money on frivolous items. Establishing a savings strategy early in life can have a significant impact on your financial future because it allows you to capitalize on the power of compound interest. Whether you're saving for a car, college, or just a rainy day, automating your savings is a great method to accumulate wealth over time.

Set financial goals: Setting financial goals will help you stay motivated and focused on your long-term financial goals. Having precise goals in mind will allow you to manage your money effectively whether you're saving or spending.

Avoid debt: Debt can be a major obstacle to responsible money management. Try to avoid taking on debt for unnecessary purchases and pay off any existing debt as quickly as possible.

Prioritize needs over wants: Prioritizing what you need over what you want is a crucial component of efficient money management as a teen. Needs such as food, housing, and healthcare are necessary for your survival and well-being. In contrast, wants are things that you desire even though they aren't strictly necessary. When managing your money, it's critical to prioritize your necessities over your wants since this ensures that you have enough money to handle your vital expenses. Although it's normal to want to spend money on things that provide you pleasure or happiness, it's prudent to first ensure that you have enough money to satisfy your basic needs. This perspective will help you stay within your budget and ensure that you can care for yourself in the long run. It doesn't mean you can't enjoy the occasional treat or splurge on something you really desire, but it does require you to be conscious of your spending patterns.

Review your finances regularly: Regularly reviewing your finances is another important technique for managing your money effectively. It's important to have a clear understanding of your income, expenses, and financial goals and regularly go over your budget to ensure that you're on track. By reviewing your finances regularly, you'll be able to see areas where you're spending too much and improve on it. You can also identify opportunities to save more money, such as finding ways to reduce your monthly bills or taking advantage of discounts or promotions. Regularly reviewing your finances can also help you stay motivated and focused on your financial goals.

By using these techniques, you can take control of your spending and saving and work toward achieving your financial goals.

BUDGETING AND SAVING

Budgeting is the process of making a strategy to manage your money. It involves assessing your income and expenses and allocating your money to several areas such as groceries or entertainment. The purpose of budgeting is to verify that you aren't overspending and confirm that you're living within your means.

Saving, on the other hand, involves putting a portion of your earnings aside for future use. This could include putting money aside for emergencies, saving for a large purchase, or investing for retirement. Saving enables you to plan for unexpected expenses and attain your long-term financial objectives.

Budgeting and saving are two crucial parts of personal finance management that frequently go hand in hand. Finding areas where you can cut back on spending and save more money is much easier with a prepared budget. Similarly, by saving money, you can increase your financial cushion and have more flexibility in your budget.

Saving is essential because it allows you to build up an emergency fund that you may use to meet unforeseen expenses. These could include medical expenditures, car repairs, or any other expenses that pop up unexpectedly. You can avoid going into debt to cover these expenses if you have an emergency fund. Saving also teaches you the value of delayed gratification. Instead of spending all your money at once, you learn to save for larger investments or long-term goals.

Finally, budgeting and saving can assist you in gaining financial independence. You can lessen your dependency on your parents or guardians for financial support by taking charge of your finances and making prudent spending decisions. This can be uplifting and make you feel more secure in your future abilities to manage your finances.

ACTIVITY: CREATING A BUDGET

Here are some steps you can follow to create a budget of your own and categorize your income, expenses, and financial obligations:

- **Determine your income:** If you work part time or receive a monthly allowance, you need to first figure out how much money you get at the end of each month.
- **Track expenses:** Make note of all your spending, especially fixed expenses such as your phone bill or transportation, but also variable expenses like entertainment.
- **Prioritize expenses:** After making a list of your expenses, determine which costs are necessary and which are optional.
- **Limit your discretionary spending:** Set limits on how much you can spend on things like entertainment or eating out.

- **Save up:** Set aside some of your income for the future, whether it's for a specific goal or just for rainy days. Every little bit helps!

CHAPTER NINE: DIVERSITY AND INCLUSION

Diversity and inclusion are two concepts that have become increasingly important in the world today. In straightforward terms, diversity refers to the differences between people due to gender, race, religion, age, ethnicity, or other traits. On the other hand, inclusion refers to creating a safe and welcoming environment for all individuals regardless of their differences.

Understanding and embracing diversity and inclusion are crucial for building a healthy and thriving society. This appreciation is what will help you recognize and appreciate the unique qualities and perspectives that each individual brings to the table. When you value diversity and promote inclusion, you create a sense of belonging and foster a culture of acceptance, love, empathy, and respect for all.

As you read on, you'll learn more about the importance of diversity and inclusion. You will see what it means to be inclusive and how you, as a teenager, can be a part of a thriving society where diversity is celebrated and inclusion is the status quo. This chapter will also address some common misconceptions about these principles and provide tips for promoting diversity and inclusion in your own life and community.

WHY DIVERSITY AND INCLUSION ARE IMPORTANT

Diversity and inclusion create a more welcoming and accommodating environment where everyone feels safe, respected, and valued. They also promote a sense of belonging, which is crucial for building healthy and thriving communities.

Suppose you observe that your society, school, or friends don't value diversity and promote inclusion. In that case, individuals are excluded from the group and denied the opportunity to contribute to their full potential. This not only harms those excluded but also limits the potential of people from marginalized backgrounds.

Everyone deserves to be treated with respect and dignity. Learning about the cultures, ideas, and viewpoints of the people you interact with is a key step. It's also important to actively seek out other opinions and be receptive to differing points of view.

Another step you want to consider is checking your own biases. Whether you're conscious of them or not, everyone is biased in some way. It's critical to identify ways in which you may be biased and actively seek to eliminate those prejudices before they cost you essential friendships. Looking at your own life, examining your views and presumptions, looking for different viewpoints, and being open to learning and development can all contribute to this.

EMBRACING DIVERSITY AND INCLUSION

Now that you understand the importance of diversity and inclusion, let's discuss some strategies for embracing and promoting inclusion in your life and your relationships.

Educate Yourself

One of the most essential strategies for embracing diversity is to educate yourself. This means learning about different cultures, beliefs, and experiences. You can do this by reading books, talking to people you know, watching documentaries, or attending cultural events in your community.

Check your biases: We all have biases whether we realize it or not. Recognizing and challenging them is essential to creating a more inclusive environment. This can involve actively seeking diverse perspectives, challenging stereotypes, and being open to different viewpoints.

Create a safe space: Creating a safe space is essential for promoting inclusion. This means creating an environment where everyone feels welcome and valued. You can do this by actively listening to others, respecting everyone, and being mindful of your language and behavior.

Celebrate diversity: Celebrating diversity can involve recognizing and valuing the differences between people and embracing the unique perspectives and experiences everyone brings to the table. You can celebrate diversity by attending cultural events, trying new foods, or learning a new language.

Be proactive: Finally, it's essential to be proactive in promoting diversity and inclusion. This can involve advocating for certain policies, volunteering with organizations that promote diversity and inclusion, or simply being a positive role model by treating others with respect and dignity.

In essence, accepting and embracing diversity and promoting inclusion are essential strategies for creating a peaceful society where teenagers like you can thrive without hate toward other people. Diversity and inclusion are how you create a more equitable and just society for all.

STANDING UP TO DISCRIMINATION

Imagine that you're at the airport and you see a person of color being harassed at the checkpoint while every other person passes without being stopped. You wait a little longer to observe, and you realize that the only passengers asked to step aside and have their bags checked are people of color. What comes to your mind? What do you think is happening? What would your reaction be in a situation like that?

Discrimination is a serious issue that affects many people, and it's essential to stand up against it. Discrimination can take many forms, including racism, sexism, homophobia, and ableism. Whatever the form, discrimination is harmful and has no place in a fair and just society.

First and foremost, standing up to discrimination is simply the right and moral thing to do. Discrimination is a form of oppression that can lead to actual harm to marginalized individuals and communities. Standing up against discrimination can help create a more equitable and just society where everyone is treated with respect and dignity.

When you stand up and speak up against discrimination, you're also helping those who are targeted by it. Discrimination can profoundly impact people's lives, causing them to feel isolated, unwelcome, and undervalued.

Standing up against discrimination also sends a powerful message to those around you. It shows that discrimination isn't acceptable and that people are committed to fighting against bias. This message can inspire others to act.

Finally, standing up against discrimination can create change. By speaking out against discrimination and advocating for policies that promote equity and inclusion, you can help create a more just and equitable society. This can involve working with community organizations where you live, contacting elected officials, or simply speaking out when you see discrimination happening. You could also volunteer to lend your voice online.

Embracing Different Cultures and Backgrounds

One way to embrace different cultures and backgrounds is to seek new experiences. By exposing yourself to new cultures, you'll learn about the world around you and gain a greater appreciation for the diversity that's present all over the world.

Another way to embrace different cultures and backgrounds is to challenge yourself to step outside your comfort zone. This might mean volunteering at a community center that serves a different population than you're used to or learning a new language to better communicate with people from different cultures. When you put yourself in unfamiliar situations, you'll learn about new cultures and gain confidence in your ability to adapt to different situations.

Traveling is also a great and fun-filled way to gain cultural sensitivity. You'll become more well rounded and empathetic by seeing that your view of the world isn't the only one.

Creating a Culture of Inclusion in Your School and Beyond

Creating a culture of inclusion takes effort and commitment from everyone involved. As a member of your community, there are steps you can take to promote inclusion and create a welcoming environment for everyone around you.

One fundamental way to encourage inclusion is to get involved in your school or community. This might mean joining a club or organization that promotes diversity and inclusion or attending events where you can share ideas and interact with peers.

Another way to create a culture of inclusion is to speak up when you see or hear something that goes against these values. This might mean challenging a friend who makes discriminatory comments or reporting bullying or harassment to a teacher or authority figure.

It's also important to be open and accepting of others' differences. This means not making assumptions about people based on race, gender, sexual orientation, or other characteristics and avoiding stereotypes and prejudices. When you approach each person with an open mind and a willingness to learn, you'll create a more welcoming and inclusive environment for everyone.

ACTIVITY: EXPLORING A NEW CULTURE THROUGH FOOD

One of the best ways to learn about a new culture is through their cuisine. Food is an essential part of any culture, and trying new dishes can help you gain a deeper appreciation for different communities' traditions, customs, and values. In this activity, we'll explore a new culture by trying some of their traditional dishes.

Choose a culture: Choose a culture you're interested in learning more about. It could be from a different part of the world or a subculture within your community. Research the culture and its culinary traditions. List a few dishes you'd like to try.

Find a restaurant or recipe: Once you've identified some dishes you'd like to try, the next step is to find a restaurant that serves them or a recipe you can follow.

Try the food: Whether you're eating at a restaurant or cooking at home, take the time to savor the flavors and textures of the dishes. Think about how they compare to the foods you're used to eating, and try to identify the unique ingredients and cooking techniques used in the cuisine. After you've finished your meal, take some time to reflect on what you've learned about that culture through its food.

Share your experience: You can write about it in a blog, create a social media post, or simply tell your friends and family about what you learned. Sharing your experience can help promote a greater understanding and appreciation for different cultures and cuisines.

CHAPTER TEN:
GROWTH MINDSET

It's easy to get discouraged when facing problems or learning new skills, but when you adopt the right perspective, every challenge turns into an opportunity for improvement. *Growth mindset* is a term used to describe a way of looking at the world. It's not a hard set of rules but more of a philosophy for approaching most things in life. The idea behind it is that everything can improve with practice over time. This is the opposite of a fixed mindset, which causes people to see themselves as permanently good or bad at something.

By approaching your weaknesses with a growth mindset, you can improve anything in your life. For example, if math isn't naturally easy for you, instead of saying "I'm not good at math," you would say, "If I practice math more, I will eventually understand it." There is actual science behind the growth mindset as well; our brains contain neurons that make up networks. These networks grow stronger each time we use them.

In this chapter, we'll explore some different strategies and techniques for developing a growth mindset. Whether you're struggling with a particular subject in school or looking to improve your overall attitude, these tips can help you shift your perspective.

HOW TO DEVELOP
A GROWTH MINDSET

Embrace challenges: Instead of shying away from challenges, see them as an opportunity to improve. When faced with a difficult task, try breaking it down into smaller, more manageable steps and tackling them individually. You'll build resilience and confidence in your abilities by facing challenges head on.

Practice self-reflection: It's a good idea to think about your strengths and weaknesses. In what areas do you excel? Where do you struggle? Use this self-awareness to identify areas where you can grow and improve. During this process, try to identify anything that falls under a fixed mindset. Anytime you think you can't do something or you're not good at it, take note. These are areas to practice a growth mindset.

Learn from mistakes: Nobody's perfect, and everyone makes mistakes from time to time. Instead of dwelling on your mistakes, focus on how they can work in your favor. Reflect on what went wrong, identify improvement areas, and plan how to improve next time. Instead of dwelling on what you didn't accomplish, concentrate on what you learned.

Cultivate a positive mindset: Practice gratitude, focus on things you can control, and challenge negative self-talk. Surround yourself with positive influences. If this is difficult, ask other people to help you see the good in the situation. Sometimes, it's easier to be objective from an outside standpoint.

Emphasize effort over talent: Instead of focusing on innate talent or abilities, consider the importance of hard work. Recognize that progress takes time and dedication and that there aren't any shortcuts to success. By valuing effort over talent, you become more likely to see challenges as a good thing and push yourself to learn and grow.

LEARNING FROM FAILURES

Throughout your life, you will inevitably encounter failure. Some people will use this as a reason to quit, but if you give up, you miss out on improvement and eventual mastery. Here are some tips for transforming your perceived failures into lessons:

Change your mindset: Changing your attitude is a huge step in learning. Start seeing failure as a necessary step toward success. This will assist you in developing resilience, perseverance, and a sense of empowerment.

Set realistic goals: Many people try to make too many big changes all at once and then find themselves discouraged or overwhelmed. Setting realistic goals helps you stay committed and motivated to achieve them. If you fail at something, sometimes you just need to break the goal down into a smaller step.

Practice perseverance: To persevere is to keep pursuing your goal, despite difficulty or delay, until you succeed. Even if you take a little time before trying again, don't wait too long to get back to your goal. Nearly everything you've already learned has only come with multiple attempts. Think about a child learning to walk. They will fall multiple times before they're strong enough to stand unassisted. It's all part of the process, and perseverance is what keeps you going despite setbacks.

Ask for help: Being willing to ask for help is essential if you want to succeed in numerous areas of life. No one person knows everything, and sometimes you need assistance from other people to achieve your goals or overcome challenges. Asking for help can save you time and energy, prevent mistakes, and provide new insights. However, asking for help can also be challenging, especially if you feel afraid of being judged or rejected. To overcome these barriers, it's important to cultivate self-awareness and identify your needs and limitations. Be clear in your requests, choose the right person to ask, and communicate your gratitude and willingness to reciprocate. By asking for help when you need it, you will improve your chances of success, strengthen your relationships, and contribute to a culture of mutual support and collaboration.

ACTIVITY: TRY SOMETHING NEW

Challenge yourself to try a new hobby or skill that you've always been interested in but haven't tried yet. Here's how you can get started:

- **Choose a hobby or skill:** This could be anything from writing to playing an instrument to coding.
- **Research the requirements:** You might certain supplies, equipment, or online resources. Pick something financially feasible. If you don't have a part-time job, the cost of in-person lessons might not be reasonable. That's okay! You

can always work toward those goals later. For now, pick something you can start immediately.

- **Set aside time to practice:** Begin with a short session of 15 to 30 minutes. Slowly increase as you become more comfortable and consistent.
- **Find a supportive community:** Try to meet others who are also trying out this hobby or skill. You might be able to find a local group, an online platform, or even some friends who are interested in the same thing.
- **See what's available online:** If you have a social media platform or can access videos online, start watching and following people who are already involved in your new hobby.

By taking on this challenge, you will not only learn a new hobby or skill, but you'll also build confidence and start to develop a growth mindset. You might even discover a new passion that you never knew existed.

CHAPTER ELEVEN:
SOCIAL MEDIA
AND TECHNOLOGY

Social media and technology have become everyday parts of our lives. People worldwide use different platforms to connect, communicate, and share information. While social media has undoubtedly brought people closer together and provided new opportunities for networking and collaboration, it has also been linked to negative outcomes such as anxiety and depression, cyberbullying, and a decrease in face-to-face social interaction.

Similarly, technology has transformed the way humans live, work, and study, but it has also raised worries about privacy, security, and the impact of automation on jobs. As you continue to navigate this rapidly changing world, it's crucial to approach social media and technology carefully, keeping both the benefits and drawbacks of these powerful tools in mind. However, if used with proper caution, they can be safe the vast majority of the time.

Cyberbullying, online harassment, identity theft, and exposure to inappropriate content are all concerns linked with social media. The use of technology can also be physically dangerous in certain situations, such as when driving, operating heavy machinery, or in other circumstances where it could distract you from important tasks. It's important to be aware of these possible dangers and take precautions. This should involve setting time limits, practicing good digital hygiene, and getting help when necessary.

SOCIAL MEDIA, TECHNOLOGY, AND MENTAL HEALTH

Social media and technology have had a tremendous impact on teenagers' mental health. These platforms have opened up new communication channels and methods of self-expression and enjoyment. Excessive use of social media and technology, however, has been related to various unfavorable mental health outcomes.

One of the most noticeable consequences of social media and technology is that they can add to feelings of worry, despair, and low self-esteem. When you compare your life with images and posts that seem to depict others' lives as perfect, you may start to feel inadequate and insecure. Excessive screen time can also disrupt your sleep patterns and exacerbate negative feelings.

If you've noticed that you spend more time engaging with devices than socializing with classmates in person, consider that this can contribute to social isolation. It might result in feelings of loneliness and alienation, negatively influencing your mental health.

Cyberbullying has been on the rise recently as well, and social media and technology have made it easier for bullies to harass others. This can have serious psychological effects on victims, such as anxiety, depression, and, in some cases, suicide.

Finally, excessive use of social media and technology has been related to addiction-like behavior, which can severely impact mental health. You must establish good habits and boundaries with technology to offset these potential detrimental consequences.

USING SOCIAL MEDIA AND TECHNOLOGY IN A HEALTHY WAY

Here are some strategies for leveraging social media and technology to your advantage:

Setting boundaries: First and foremost, you must learn to apply limits to your screen time. In your use of social media, determine how much time you want to spend online and stick to it. Set aside specific times of day for checking your social media accounts, and avoid checking them before bedtime or in the middle of the night. Setting boundaries is a fundamental method of managing social media usage. It means recognizing the triggers that lead to excessive use, setting goals, and limiting the time you spend on social media. Techniques such as website blockers can help you stay consistent with the boundaries you set. Take regular breaks from social media, communicate boundaries with family and friends, and turn off notifications when it's time for a break. By implementing these tactics, you can control your social media use and keep it from interfering with other elements of your life.

Reset from technology: You should periodically take a longer hiatus from social media and technology. Take a walk, read a book, or do something that doesn't involve a screen. Most people check social media habitually as part of their daily routines. However, if this practice affects your mental health, one simple remedy is to stop. You only need to delete the app, not necessarily your account. Fill the time you normally spend on social media with other things you enjoy, such as reading, playing sports, or watching a movie. When you feel ready, you can reinstall the apps on your device if you want.

Be cautious: Be careful with the information you give about yourself on the internet. Avoid including your location in posts, and be mindful of what you disclose. For example, it's wise to wait before you've returned from an event or trip before telling others about it. Recognize that you have a digital footprint that will follow you across the internet and that anything you post will be added to it.

Prioritize real-life connections: Make a conscious effort to interact with your peers in person or over the phone. Plan social gatherings, get-togethers, or dates that don't involve social media or technology. It's easy to become lost in social media and online interactions in today's digital world, but it's critical to prioritize in-person friendships. Physically spending time with friends and family can provide invaluable possibilities for personal development, emotional support, and meaningful relationships. Scheduling time for social activities like going out to eat or participating in group activities is essential. These activities can help you form stronger bonds, create memories, and improve your mental health. Even little things like saying hi to neighbors or coworkers creates real-life bonds. You can build a sense of belonging, lessen feelings of isolation, and increase general well-being by prioritizing in-person interaction.

Embrace quiet time: Turning off notifications for social media apps and emails will reduce how often you're distracted. When notifications are enabled, each new like, repost, or message can interrupt what you're doing, causing you to check your phone or social network account. This behavior can quickly become addictive and disrupt other aspects of your life. Avoiding distractions can boost productivity, lower stress, and improve work-life balance.

Use technology for good: When used correctly, the internet can be a very beneficial tool. It gives users access to knowledge and resources on various topics, ranging from instructional materials to current events and entertainment. You can broaden your view of the world by using the internet to study and learn about things that interest you. The internet can also be utilized to interact with people who share similar interests through online communities, forums, and social media groups. This can give you a sense of belonging and help you obtain support and assistance when you face personal difficulties. The internet can also be used to express yourself creatively and showcase talents, particularly through blogging, vlogging, or creating digital art.

By employing these strategies, you can utilize social media and technology in a healthy and balanced manner that adds to, rather than detracts from, your life.

ELIMINATING NEGATIVE INFLUENCES

As a teenager, you're at a vulnerable stage in life where you may face various negative influences that can affect your behavior, attitudes, and decision-making. Here are some steps that can help you identify and eliminate negative influences:

Figure out the source: The first step is to pinpoint the source of the harmful effects. This could be an individual, a group, a behavior, or an environment. Consider whether this influence is consistent with your values and ambitions.

Evaluate the impact: The next stage is to assess the bad influence's impact on your life. Is it making you worried, depressed, or stressed? Is it causing you to participate in dangerous or harmful behaviors? Does it impede your academic or personal development?

Seek positive alternatives: After identifying the negative influence and its impact, look for positive alternatives that are consistent with your beliefs and aspirations. Surround yourself with good role models; participate in groups or activities that interest you; and seek help from friends, family, or counselors.

Practice self-care: Taking care of yourself physically, mentally, and emotionally is important. Eat a healthy diet, sleep well, exercise regularly, and engage in activities that bring you joy and fulfillment. Self-care is an essential component of your overall well-being. Prioritizing activities that improve physical, emotional, and mental wellness is critical. For example, getting enough sleep each night is one way to practice self-care. Adequate sleep aids in the recovery of the body and mind, making it easier for you to deal with daily challenges. A balanced diet can also offer nutrients that energize the body and support overall health. Mindfulness practices such as meditation, yoga, and deep breathing exercises can calm the mind and enhance attention. Making time for fun things, such as hobbies or spending time with friends and family, can promote a positive mindset and general happiness.

Take time to reflect: Reflect on your choices and actions and how they align with your values and goals. Take responsibility for your own behavior and make choices that reflect your true self and aspirations. As a teenager, it's critical to reflect on the decisions you make. Reflection involves reviewing previous decisions and activities to identify what worked and what didn't. This process allows you to learn from your mistakes and make better future decisions. It's vital to accept responsibility for your decisions and understand the consequences of those choices. Journaling, talking with a trusted friend or mentor, or simply taking time to think about your behavior are all ways to reflect. Examining your choices allows you to better define your values and priorities, which will enable you to make decisions that are consistent with your goals. By reflecting on your choices, you'll gain valuable insights and be able to recognize and eliminate harmful influences.

ACTIVITY: DIGITAL DETOX CHALLENGE

This activity requires you to disconnect from technology and social media for a set period of time in order to focus on other things. Unplugging and taking a break from technology can be quite good for your mental health. While it may be challenging at first, a break like this can provide a much-needed mental respite from the continual stimulation of your devices. You may find that you have more time and energy to devote to other activities that you enjoy, and you just might discover new hobbies or pastimes that you wish to explore further. It's kind of an extreme version of setting boundaries in which you track and analyze how much time you spend on social media. Ensure you do this challenge with one or more of your friends or peers. It will help you be accountable and achieve your desired result.

Avoid using your cell phone except out of necessity. Do this for a day, a week, or more; it depends on how long you want to engage in this challenge. With technology's constant availability, it can be tough to unplug and disconnect from social media and technological devices. You may reduce your dependence on technology and the negative effects associated with excessive use, such as eye strain, headaches, and lower productivity, by limiting the use of a cell phone to only essential tasks.

Avoid watching TV. After a long day, many people turn to their televisions for amusement and to unwind. However, excessively watching television can contribute to physical inactivity, poor academic achievement, and even a lack of social skills. During this challenge, limit your television to educational shows and the news. Educational programs provide you with vital knowledge and insights, while news shows keep you up to date on current events.

Avoid the excessive use of laptops and computers. It's often difficult to avoid using laptops and computers since much of what you do at school requires a computer. However, you need to be aware of how much time you spend using these gadgets outside of school and take steps to restrict their use. Long-term usage of laptops and computers has been linked to eye strain, migraines, and even carpal tunnel syndrome. Excessive use of technology can disrupt sleep patterns, thus impacting your general health and well-being.

Avoid gaming devices. While PC gaming and handheld devices can be enjoyable forms of entertainment, it's important to be aware of the potentially harmful effects of excessive gaming. Excessive gaming can cause eye strain, migraines, and even neck problems. Some people are also prone to hyperfixation, which can cause you to spend a large amount of your time on an activity without even realizing it. To avoid these detrimental effects, restrict your gaming time and balance it with physical activity or social connection. Take frequent breaks to stretch and rest your eyes. You can follow these steps to enjoy the pleasures of gaming without jeopardizing your general health and well-being.

Spend time with loved ones in person. Spending time with friends and family is essential for developing strong relationships and cultivating a sense of community. In today's digital society, disconnecting from phones and technological devices is getting increasingly difficult. It's critical to consider the potentially harmful impacts of excessive electronic device use on your relationships and mental health. To avoid these consequences, make an effort to spend meaningful time in person with friends and family away from phones and technological gadgets. This can include activities such as outdoor games, athletics, or simply sharing a meal together.

Read a book. Reading a hard-copy book can be a great technique to practice digital detoxing while also promoting mental health and well-being. Many individuals have moved to reading books on electronic devices such as e-readers and tablets. While these devices have their advantages, reading a printed book can give a more tactile and immersive experience, allowing you to focus on the present moment. Reading a hard-copy book can also encourage relaxation by reducing stress and anxiety. Reading has been shown to boost cognitive function, broaden your knowledge and vocabulary, and even foster empathy and understanding.

Write in a journal. Keeping a journal can be an effective way to create a stronger sense of self-awareness by taking the time to reflect on your thoughts and feelings. This can help you better understand your own thoughts and feelings and those of others. Journaling can also help you cope with stress and anxiety by allowing you to express your emotions and work through challenging experiences.

Practice meditation. Use this time to concentrate on your breathing and become more present in the moment. There are numerous applications and guided meditations available to help you get started. Meditation allows you to unplug from technological gadgets and focus on the present moment, making it an effective method of digital detox. You can reduce tension and anxiety, improve mental clarity, and create a stronger sense of self-awareness by practicing meditation.

Exercise or practice yoga. Physical activity is an excellent way to reduce stress and enhance your overall health. Enroll in a new fitness class or go for a run outside. By exercising, you can limit your screen time and combat the negative effects of physical inactivity, eye strain, and headaches that can result from using devices. Exercise has also been demonstrated to improve mental health by lowering stress, increasing self-esteem, and improving cognitive performance.

After doing this challenge, do you plan to reduce your screen time again in the future or not? Did you find it difficult to disconnect from technology? What did you enjoy about taking a break from social media and technology? Did you discover any new hobbies or activities that you would like to pursue? Reflect on your experiences by taking the following steps:

- Write about your experience in your journal and share it with your friends or peers.
- Share the challenges you faced with your friends.
- Share how you benefited from a digital detox.

Taking this challenge seriously will grant you a better understanding of how to navigate your relationships with your peers, manage technology and social media, and make positive changes to improve your overall well-being.

CHAPTER TWELVE: DEVELOPING RESILIENCE

In this chapter, you'll learn what it means to get going when the going gets tough. Between school, friends, family, and everything else going on in your life, it's easy to feel overwhelmed and burned out. But here's the thing: No matter what life throws your way, you have the power to bounce back and come out even stronger than before.

Resilience is the ability to cope with and adapt to difficult situations, ranging from getting a bad grade to something more serious like a family crisis. Having resilience doesn't mean that you're invincible or that you'll never feel beaten or lost; it just means you have the willpower and mindset to overcome challenges and keep moving forward.

This chapter will cover some key strategies and habits that can help you develop resilience as a teen. From building a strong support network to practicing self-care and mindfulness, there are plenty of things you can do to boost your resilience and learn to thrive in the face of adversity.

THE IMPORTANCE OF RESILIENCE

Sometimes, life can feel like a roller coaster with ups and downs that can leave you feeling dizzy and disoriented. That's why it's so important to develop resilience as a teen. Resilience is like a mental and emotional safety net that catches you when you fall and helps you bounce back up on your feet stronger than before.

Here are a few reasons why resilience is such an important trait:

Coping with stress: Life can be stressful at times, but with resilience, you can develop the ability to manage stress rather than letting it overwhelm you. Resilience makes you better equipped to handle challenges and setbacks without feeling like everything is falling apart.

Boosting your confidence: Every time you overcome a tough situation, you strengthen your ability to manage future challenges. Resilience helps you believe in yourself and keep a positive perspective. The next time things get hard, take a moment to consider all the bad days and frustrations you've already survived.

Achieving your goals: Resilience and perseverance go hand in hand. Resilience gives you the power and motivation to persevere after a setback. This is one of the key steps to achieving a goal when things are difficult.

HOW TO DEVELOP RESILIENCE

Developing resilience as a teen isn't always easy, but it's definitely worth the effort. Luckily, there are plenty of techniques available to build resilience and become more equipped to handle life's challenges. Here are a few techniques to get you started:

Create a strong support system: Surrounding yourself with people who love and care about you creates a great source of courage and solace. Maintaining your bonds with loved ones, friends, and mentors ensures that you have a support network for tough times.

Practice self-care: Self-care includes caring for your physical, mental, and emotional needs. This can involve getting enough sleep, maintaining a healthy diet, exercising frequently, and participating in enjoyable and relaxing activities.

Develop a growth mindset: Resilience is all about having a growth attitude, which involves viewing setbacks as opportunities for development. Try to reframe failures as opportunities to grow and learn rather than being demoralized by them.

Practice mindfulness: Mindfulness is a method that can help you avoid dwelling on anxieties about the past or the future and instead stay anchored in the present. There are several ways to practice mindfulness, including deep breathing exercises, meditation, and focusing on your senses and the environment.

Developing resilience is a process that takes time and effort, but by using these techniques and others like them, you can become more equipped to handle whatever life throws your way.

PERSEVERANCE
AND GRIT

Perseverance is about staying committed to your goals and not giving up even when things get tough. Grit is the combination of passion and perseverance over a long period that helps you develop strength of character. It's the ability to maintain your focus and work hard for an extended period despite setbacks and distractions.

Why are perseverance and grit so important for teens like you? Let's explore a few key reasons.

Overcoming obstacles: There are many difficulties and challenges in life. Perseverance and grit give you the fortitude and resolve to meet challenges head on, whether they're related to a challenging school project, a sporting loss, or personal struggles. Instead of giving up, you learn to view challenges as chances for development and devise innovative solutions to get through them.

Achieving long-term goals: Most worthwhile goals require time and effort. Perseverance and tenacity are essential for sticking with your goals. These traits support you in maintaining concentration, overcoming obstacles, and making steady advancements toward your goals.

Developing character and discipline: Grit and perseverance help create crucial character traits like resilience, self-control, and determination. Developing these traits improves your capacity to persevere under pressure, put in long hours, and overcome obstacles in various contexts.

Perseverance and grit aren't about being perfect or never experiencing setbacks. They allow you to embrace challenges, learn from failure, and stay committed to your goals. By developing these qualities, you empower yourself to grow, achieve, and positively impact your own life and the world around you.

Staying Strong Through Ups and Downs

How can you weather the good times and the bad without getting too shaken up? Here are some tips:

Find coping strategies: Everyone has ways of coping with stress and difficult emotions. Some people find comfort in music, art, or exercise, while others prefer writing or talking. Experiment with different coping strategies to find what works best for you.

Practice self-compassion: It's easy to be hard on yourself when things don't go as planned. But practicing self-compassion — treating yourself with kindness and understanding — can help you bounce back from setbacks. Remember that everyone makes mistakes and it's okay to be imperfect.

Building resilience takes time and practice. Don't be too hard on yourself if you're not feeling resilient immediately. With patience and persistence, you can develop the skills you need to stay strong through life's ups and downs.

The Resilience Toolbox: Tips and Tricks for Handling Stress and Pressure

If you're reading this, chances are you're looking for tips on handling stress and pressure. Well, you've come to the right place! Here are some best practices for building resilience:

Take a break: When you're feeling overwhelmed, sometimes the best thing you can do is take a break. Step away from whatever is causing you stress and do something that relaxes you. Walk outside, listen to your favorite music, or read a book. Giving yourself a break can recharge your batteries and allow you to come back stronger.

Practice positive self-talk: How you talk to yourself can greatly impact how you feel. Try to replace negative thoughts with positive ones. Instead of thinking *I can't do this*, change your perspective: *I can do this; I just need to take it one step at a time.*

Prioritize self-care: Taking care of yourself is essential for building resilience. Ensure you're getting enough sleep, eating well, and doing things that make you happy. It's not selfish to prioritize your well-being — it's necessary to stay strong.

Try deep breathing: Deep breathing can help you feel calmer and more centered when you're feeling stressed. Try taking a few slow, deep breaths through your nose and out through your mouth.

Practice gratitude: Focusing on what you're grateful for can help shift your mindset to a more positive place. Take a few minutes each day to think about what you're thankful for or write it down in a journal.

Find your support system: Building a support system with friends, family, or a therapist can help you feel less alone during tough times. Reach out and ask for help when you need it.

Building resilience takes time and practice. You won't become an expert overnight, but every step you take is progress. Over time, you'll feel stronger and more capable of handling whatever life throws your way.

ACTIVITY: TRYING A NEW PHYSICAL CHALLENGE

Physical challenges are an excellent way to practice and develop your resilience, perseverance, and grit. They give you the opportunity to push your boundaries and discover your physical and mental strengths. Here's how to get started:

- **Choose a physical activity:** This could be anything from rock climbing to yoga, martial arts to dance, or any other physical activity that excites you.

- **Research and learn about the activity:** Look for online tutorials, instructional videos, and articles to help you understand the basics so that you can get started.

- **Set a goal and create a plan:** Decide what you want to achieve through the activity and create a plan for how you will approach it. Break it down into smaller achievable steps, and make a timeline or schedule for yourself.

- **Get started:** Start practicing the activity and working toward your goal. Be patient with yourself, and remember that it's okay to make mistakes and encounter setbacks.

- **Reflect on your experience:** After you've completed the physical challenge, take some time to reflect on your experience. What did you learn about yourself? What challenges did you face, and how did you overcome them? What new skills or strengths did you develop? Use these insights to further build your resilience, perseverance, and grit.

Remember to choose a physical activity that's safe and appropriate for your skill level, and always seek professional guidance or supervision if necessary. With this activity, you'll develop your physical abilities and build your mental and emotional resilience, perseverance, and grit. Have fun trying something new!

CHAPTER THIRTEEN: PLANNING FOR THE FUTURE

You might feel like you have all the time in the world to figure out what you want to do with your life, but it's never too early to start planning for the future. Whether you want to go to college, start a career, or travel the world, having a plan in place can help you achieve your goals and live the life you want. Have you ever thought about why the future scares so many people? It's because they have a fear of uncertainty. They can't tell what awaits them, so the thought of it terrifies them.

In this chapter, you will gain an understanding of why you have to plan for the future and learn how to create a plan that will work for you. This chapter will cover everything from setting goals and making an action plan to staying motivated and overcoming obstacles. Grab a notebook and pen, and let's get started on planning for your bright future!

THE VALUE OF PLANNING AHEAD

It's easy to get caught up in the moment and forget about the future. However, it's important to recognize the significance of planning ahead if you want to achieve your goals and live the life you desire for yourself.

First and foremost, planning for your future is how you set and achieve your goals, especially the long-term ones. With a plan in place, you'll know exactly what you need to do to achieve your goals, and you can take modest actions each day to get there. Having a plan can help you stay focused and motivated, whether you want to go to college, start a business, or explore the world.

Life is unpredictable, and unexpected events can occur at any time in your life. However, when you have a strategy, you may foresee future challenges and be able to devise solutions to them before it's dire. This will empower you to stand firm in the face of adversity and achieve your goals even when things get tricky. Create plans that include alternatives for when the going gets tough.

Another reason that making plans for your future is important is that it allows you to make better judgments in the present. When you know where you want to go in life, you'll make decisions that are consistent with your long-term goals and values. This can help you avoid temptations and distractions that might otherwise derail your progress.

Finally, making plans can build confidence and self-esteem. When you have a plan, you know you're in control of your life and actively working toward your objectives. This could make you feel more secure in your talents and empowered to live your chosen life.

HOW TO SET AND ACHIEVE FUTURE GOALS

Typically, teenagers have big dreams and aspirations for their future, but it can be challenging to know where to start. Setting and achieving future goals requires planning, commitment, and perseverance. This section will introduce you to some strategies that will help you set and achieve your future goals.

Define your goals: The first step in setting and accomplishing future goals is to clearly define them. Write out your goals and why they're important to you. Ensure that your objectives are specific, measurable, achievable, important, and time bound. Defining your goals in this manner will keep you focused and motivated.

Break it down: Once your goals have been classified, break them down into smaller tasks. This will help you stay motivated and keep you from getting overwhelmed by your ambitions. Begin with more manageable goals and work your way up to the difficult ones.

Create a plan: Create a strategy for accomplishing your goals. This plan should include the steps you need to take to attain your goals as well as any roadblocks you may meet along the way. Make sure your strategy is reasonable, and be ready to make changes as needed.

Stay accountable: Share your goals with someone you trust who's more experienced than you, and urge them to hold you responsible. This could be a friend, relative, or mentor. Check in with them frequently to keep them updated on your progress and obtain input on how you can improve.

Celebrate your progress: Recognize your progress along the road. This will keep you motivated and give you the courage to work toward your goals. Celebrate your accomplishments no matter how minor they may seem.

Keep an optimistic attitude: Achieving your future goals will involve hard work and devotion, but it's possible to reach your dreams. Don't get discouraged by setbacks or barriers. Maintain your focus and keep moving forward.

Developing and achieving future goals requires preparation, dedication, and tenacity. With the right mindset, you can fulfill your future objectives and live the life you desire.

THE VALUE OF SELF-REFLECTION

Self-reflection is an important tool for personal growth and development. It allows you to examine your thoughts, feelings, and actions and gain insight into your strengths and weaknesses. Let's explore the importance of self-reflection and how it can help you become the best version of yourself.

Increased self-awareness: Self-reflection improves your self-awareness, which is the foundation of personal development and growth. You can better understand yourself and your reasoning by taking the time to think about your thoughts, feelings, and actions. This improved self-awareness will assist you in making better judgments and achieving your objectives.

Increased self-esteem: Self-reflection can boost your self-esteem. You build a sense of pride and self-worth when you focus on your successes and the positive impact you've had on others. This, in turn, will enhance your confidence and assist you in confronting new obstacles.

Improved problem-solving skills: Self-reflection can also help you improve your problem-solving skills. You can detect patterns and learn from your blunders by reviewing past experiences. This enables you to approach new difficulties from a different angle and devise more effective solutions.

Improved relationships: Self-reflection can help you strengthen your interpersonal relationships. You can discover areas for improvement and work on establishing better communication skills by reflecting on your interactions with others. This can result in more pleasant and satisfying relationships.

Greater sense of purpose: Self-reflection allows you to uncover what's genuinely important to you and connect your behaviors with your goals by reviewing your values, beliefs, and passions. This can assist you in living a more meaningful and fulfilled life.

Self-reflection is an effective instrument for personal growth and development. It enables you to become the best version of yourself and build the life you want by taking the time to reflect on your ideas, feelings, and actions.

The Role of Education in Planning for the Future

Education is an integral part of planning that you must recognize and not downplay when making plans for your future. It will provide you with the required knowledge, skills, and credentials to pursue your goals and achieve success in your chosen field. Whether you're planning to enter the workforce, learn a skill, or start your own business, a solid educational foundation is important for navigating the challenges and opportunities ahead.

When you pursue education, you learn more than just theories, facts, and figures. You also learn to think and solve challenges. Critical thinking skills are necessary for all aspects of life, and schooling is an effective way to cultivate them. Education will teach you how to examine, evaluate, and use data. These abilities are required to make sound decisions in both your personal and professional lives.

Personal development is another key advantage of schooling. When you learn something new, you broaden your horizons and develop new parts of your brain. This can help you become more imaginative and understanding. You might even uncover a new interest or talent you didn't know you possessed. Education also enables you to build confidence and develop a sense of direction.

Furthermore, education allows people from all walks of life to learn skills and knowledge that will help them succeed in life. Education is essential for facilitating social mobility and eliminating inequality. When you have equal access to education, you have an equal chance of success.

Navigating Future Uncertainty and Adapting to Change

One of the first things to remember is that change is inevitable. The world is continuously changing, and as you develop and grow, you will always face new challenges and possibilities. While change can be frightening, it can also be exciting. It allows you to experiment with new ideas, meet new people, and discover new interests.

To navigate the uncertainty of the future, it's important to concentrate on what you can control. While you can't anticipate the future, you can plan ahead to be ready for whatever comes your way. This could include creating objectives, learning new skills, or forming a support network of friends and family who can provide direction and advice.

Staying adaptive is another important component of dealing with uncertainty. Life rarely goes as planned; therefore, it's crucial to be able to pivot and adjust your plans as necessary. This could entail switching careers, discovering new interests, or taking a gap year to figure out what you want to do next.

Staying interested is one of the best strategies to staying adaptive. Keep an open mind, be eager to try new things, and cultivate curiosity. This will assist you in developing the resilience and flexibility required to manage whatever challenges may arise.

It's totally okay, desirable even, to seek assistance. No one has all the answers, and there's no shame in asking for advice and assistance from friends, family, or trusted advisors. You can navigate the uncertainties of the future and adapt to whatever changes come your way if you have the correct mindset, resources, and support network.

ACTIVITY: WRITE A LETTER TO YOUR FUTURE SELF

Writing a letter to your future self is an exciting and rewarding activity that can clarify your goals and aspirations. It's a chance to reflect on where you are now and where you want to be. Before you proceed to the steps required in this activity, here are a few reasons why you should take it seriously:

Benefits of Writing a Letter to Your Future Self

Accountability: Writing a letter to your future self can hold you accountable for achieving your goals. When you write down your aspirations, you're more likely to take action to make them a reality.

Inspiration: Reading a letter from your past self can be a powerful source of inspiration. It can remind you of your progress and motivate you to keep pushing forward.

Reflection: Writing a letter to your future self is also a chance to reflect on your current state of mind. It can help you identify areas for improvement and set realistic goals for the future.

Guide to Writing a Letter

Choose a future date: Decide on a future date when you want to read the letter. It could be a year or five years from now. Make sure to choose a date that gives you enough time to achieve your goals or at least make measurable progress.

Find a quiet place: Choose a quiet and peaceful place to write your letter. This will help you focus and collect your thoughts.

Reflect on your goals: Take some time to reflect on your current goals and aspirations. Think about what you want to achieve in the future and what steps you need to take to get there.

Write your letter: Start writing your letter to your future self. Be honest and open about your thoughts and feelings. Write about your hopes, fears, and aspirations. Be specific about what you want to achieve and how you plan to do it.

Seal your letter: Once you're done writing, seal your letter in an envelope. You can decorate the envelope with stickers or drawings to make it more personal.

Store your letter: Store it in a safe place where you won't forget about it. You could even give it to a trusted friend or family member to keep for you in a safe or locked drawer.

Open your letter: On the date you chose, open your letter and read it. Reflect on how much you've achieved and what you still want to accomplish. Use the letter as a source of inspiration to keep pushing forward toward your goals.

By following these simple steps, you can create a letter that will serve as a source of inspiration and motivation for years to come.

CONCLUSION

Having read from the first line to the last, you can testify that *Life Advice for Teens* has proven to be a comprehensive guide for teenagers who are navigating the ups and downs of life. You've read practical pieces of advice, useful tips, and insightful guidance from carefully selected topics that are relevant and important to you as a teenager in today's world.

Throughout this book, you've learned how to embrace self-discovery, growth, and change. You've likely also realized that life is full of both challenges and opportunities. By developing healthy habits, setting goals, and taking steps toward personal growth and self-improvement, you can indeed create the life you want and deserve.

This book also emphasized the importance of seeking help and support when needed. Whether it's talking to a friend, family member, or mental health professional, there is always someone who cares and is willing to listen.

Life Advice for Teens is a powerful tool that has helped other teens navigate the challenges of adolescence and beyond. It offers a roadmap for personal growth, self-improvement, and success. Now that you're willing to apply the advice and guidance from this book to your own personal situations, rest assured that you will gain a deeper understanding of yourself and the world around you.

To sum it up, *Life Advice for Teens* is a book that you can read again and again no matter where you are on your journey through life. Hopefully, you will take the advice and guidance provided in this book to heart and use it to create a fulfilling and meaningful life.

www.ingramcontent.com/pod-product-compliance
Lightning Source LLC
Chambersburg PA
CBHW060238030426

42335CB00014B/1518